THE SPECTER OF CAPITAL

Cultural Memory
in
the
Present

Hent de Vries, Editor

THE SPECTER OF CAPITAL

Joseph Vogl

Translated by Joachim Redner
and Robert Savage

STANFORD UNIVERSITY PRESS

STANFORD, CALIFORNIA

Stanford University Press
Stanford, California

The Specter of Capital was originally published in German under the title
Das Gespenst des Kapitals, © 2010, diaphanes, Zürich-Berlin.

The translation of this work was supported by a grant from the Goethe-Institut,
which is funded by the German Ministry of Foreign Affairs.

Printed in the United States of America on acid-free, archival-quality paper

Library of Congress Cataloging-in-Publication Data

Vogl, Joseph, author.
  [Gespenst des Kapitals. English]
  The specter of capital / Joseph Vogl ; translated by Joachim Redner and
Robert Savage.
      pages cm — (Cultural memory in the present)
  Translation of: Das Gespenst des Kapitals.
  Includes bibliographical references.
  ISBN 978-0-8047-8904-2 (cloth : alk. paper)
  ISBN 978-0-8047-9292-9 (pbk. : alk. paper)
    1. Capitalism. 2. Rational expectations (Economic theory).
I. Title. II. Series: Cultural memory in the present.
HB501.V57213 2014
330.12'2—dc23

                                                            2014008592

ISBN 978-0-8047-9296-7 (electronic)

Contents

Preface

Political economy has always had an affinity with spectrology, point-ing to invisible hands and other such ghostly presences to explain the course of economic events. This may well be because there is something uncanny about how, in economic processes, circulating objects and signs take on a spectral willfulness. Since the eighteenth century, market mech-anisms and the movements of capital have been experienced as mystifying phenomena, with demystification seen as the key to the achievement of enlightenment by modern societies. This is especially true for the move-ments and structures of the modern finance economy. Although financial markets can be understood as organizations in which a sizeable amount of human welfare is determined, there is nothing transparent about what takes place in them. We are referring here not only to the modes of behav-ior, mentalities, practices, or theories operative in the world of finance but also to their general dynamics, which have become a key determinant of social relations in the world today thanks to the unimaginably vast sums of money involved. Events in the world of finance shape the general course of events, so it weighs all the more heavily that there is such heated dis-agreement about the rules or logic connecting one event in this sphere with any other. The so-called crises of recent decades have led us to ask whether what is taking place in the arenas of the international finance economy is the efficient interaction of rational actors or a spectacle of the purest irrationality. In any case, it remains uncertain whether the much-invoked "spirit of capitalism" operates reliably and rationally or simply insanely.

This situation has given rise to a multifaceted problem of interpre-tation. We are dealing with an economic worldview that for some time now has presented the relationship between human beings and things in its own peculiar way; this view has in turn produced complications so intricate that economic science has taken on itself the task of elucidating them. The difficulty we are faced with, which is both real and hermeneutic, is that the science of economics has spent the last three hundred years creating the very economic facts it is now struggling to decipher. The following reflections address this state of affairs. Referring to several key constellations of economic knowledge from the eighteenth century to the present, they return repeatedly to those apparently unprecedented events—such as financial crises or "crashes"—which have rendered the workings of the finance economy anything but transparent. It is certainly not our intention to offer a blueprint for the reconstruction of the present economic system, however necessary such a task may be. Rather, our task is to understand how the modern finance economy is attempting to come to grips with the world it has created in its image. It is a world in which "the specter of capital" appears as a cipher for those powers from which our present takes its laws.

THE SPECTER OF CAPITAL

The Black Swan

Cosmopolis

It happened in New York on an April day in the year 2000. The Twin Towers of the World Trade Center were still standing. The American economy had been growing non-stop for more than a hundred months; the Dow Jones Industrial Index had just climbed above 11,000 points to reach an all-time high, while electronic trade on the NASDAQ was rallying steadily. From the top floors of the Trump World Tower, not far from UN headquarters, a view of the East River emerged as day broke, revealing the bridges and smokestacks of Queens and in the distance, beyond the suburbs, a misty haze and seagulls swarming far below.

After a sleepless night, a twenty-eight-year-old billionaire fund manager decides to leave his apartment on Manhattan's East Side to go to a hairdresser on the shabby West Side, his part of town as a child. He rides down in one of the private elevators and climbs into his white armor-plated stretch limousine, fitted out with cork sound-proofing, surveillance cameras and numerous screens relaying world news and stock exchange prices. His chiefs of security and technology are already waiting for him, along with the chauffeur. The vehicle turns into Forty-seventh Street on its way west, passing one high-rise apartment building after another. As the night wears on, it gets caught up in a series of adventures and complications that may rightly be called an odyssey.

On the way, the fund manager meets his wife and one or other of his mistresses. There is a report that the IMF director has been murdered, and likewise a Russian oligarch, a media entrepreneur, who had been a friend of this young billionaire. Crawling through the traffic, the limousine crosses Park and Madison Avenues, drives through the old Jewish neighborhood and reaches the Broadway theater district, only to be trapped in the chaos of an antiglobalization protest. A bomb explodes at the entrance to an investment bank; as a young man sets himself on fire, our speculator looks on, unaware that he himself will soon fall victim to a pie attack. Suddenly, and for no particular reason, he kills his chief of security and reaches his childhood hairdresser's near the docks. Then, equally inexplicably and abruptly, he leaves the hairdresser, gets involved with three hundred naked extras in a late-night film shoot, and coincidentally runs into his wife for the last time. An ex-colleague is waiting for him in a deserted ruin, and this man, he must finally understand, will be his murderer.

With this strange story, Don DeLillo's 2003 novel takes us right into the arena of the modern financial market, touches on the question of whether that market lends itself to narrative treatment and offers a series of narrative and rhetorical figures to represent the riddle of the finance economy, its protagonists and their operations. In his 1977 novel, *Players*, DeLillo had already pursued the question of how business finance and stock market speculation can be presented in narrative form. The narrative device he has chosen in *Cosmopolis*—a New York speculator's trip one day to the hairdresser's —amounts to a synopsis of modes of perception and problems which must still be termed capitalist. The key to this achievement is DeLillo's depiction of his main character. Around this figure he develops an allegory of modern finance capitalism, invoking both received historical ideas and contemporary economic theories. At the same time, the particular narrative method employed by the novel, with its hypertrophic amassing of events, raises fundamental questions about how different incidents are interconnected in the current global economy. An opportunity thus presents itself to question the inner workings of the capitalist economy, this system that appears to be our destiny.

Capitalist spirit

DeLillo's first move is to give his fund manager cum speculator some of the proven, canonical features that have distinguished the careers of financial and stock market speculators for at least two hundred years—and ensure that we recognize them. "Young, smart and raised by wolves" (12), renowned for the ruthless efficiency and killer instinct that make him the embodiment of finance capitalism in all its riskiness, DeLillo's hero belongs in a series running from the "condottieri," "pirates," and "were-wolves" of the money business in Balzac, through Marx's knights-errant of credit, up to the "mad dogs," "rogue traders," and "wolf packs" of today's foreign exchange markets.[1] Furthermore, DeLillo's protagonist, sporting the vigorous-sounding name of Eric Packer, enters the scene in disguise, as a character mask—or rather, a dream figure, an apparition—personifying the most recent form of finance capitalism. He is not only hyperalert and sleep-deprived, manic and prone to excess, he is at home everywhere and nowhere, an Odysseus of globalization and citizen of a monetary cosmopolis. He is marked, above all, by his longing to leave behind the ponderous heaviness of the material world, where physical conditions of ownership still prevail. He dreams that use values will die out and that the referential dimension of reality will vanish; he dreams, too, of the dissolution of the world into streams of data and the absolute tyranny of the binary code, and he places his faith in the spiritual appeal of cyber-capital, transposed into eternal light via the shimmering and flickering of charts on countless screens.

It is the dream of ultimate, radical transubstantiation. Émile Zola's novel about financial speculation, *Money*, had already referred to poets of sublime sums of money. This novel deals with a more recent mutation: Verlaine's *poète maudit* returns in a new generation of professional symbolists. Obsessive and extravagant, they devote themselves to making money "talk to itself" (77) in a free, artificial and self-referential play of signs, sealed against the rest of the world like the cork-lined office-limousine that is so reminiscent of Marcel Proust's insulated bedroom. What is finally accomplished here is nothing less than a raid by the future on the rest of time.

The words and concepts of everyday language, we are told on one occasion, are still overburdened with remnants of historical meaning: they are all too "cumbrous" and "anti-futuristic" (54). By contrast, oscillating share market and foreign exchange mechanisms dictate a rhythm, measured in nanoseconds, from which the traces of history have been erased, annulled in the maelstrom of futures and their derivatives: "The present is being sucked out of the world, to make way for a future of uncontrolled markets with huge investment potential. The future becomes urgent" (79). Just as the market is interested only in prospects for future profit, disregarding past and present, so this form of capitalism dreams of oblivion; it deals with the power of the future and fulfills itself in the end of history.

Faced with the mysteries of the most modern form of finance capitalism, DeLillo responds in his novel by combining elements of the old and the new capitalist mentality. On the one hand, this allows him to portray the addiction to change and the continual revolutionizing of global and economic structures in the name of capitalist free enterprise as a process of "creative destruction," to borrow Schumpeter's famous phrase: "Destroy the past, make the future" (93). The forces of capital were never interested in preservation; they were never "conservative" in that sense. On the other hand, it enables him to show how these forces have freed themselves from the sphere of production. Thanks to the alliance of "technology and capital" (23), the culture of the market has become as insubstantial as it is all-encompassing. The movement of capital now knows no bounds. Freed from the material manifestations of wealth, it has installed itself in "a time beyond geography and touchable money" (36). It dictates its own dynamics and standards of mobility, abandoning all local, social and political constraints.

As a result, market culture can absorb revolt and anarchy as vital expressions of its own system, treating protest as a fantasy spawned by the free market itself and capitalism as the consequential self-optimization of that fantasy: "The protest was a form of systemic hygiene. . . . It attested again, for the ten thousandth time, to market culture's innovative brilliance, its ability to reshape itself to its own flexible ends, absorbing everything around it" (99). This system, DeLillo's novel of ideas suggests, reforms itself through resistance, neutralizing opposition by assimilating whatever protest actions may spontaneously rise up against it. It achieves perfection—in keeping with the goals of "New Management"—by becoming a veritable fund of creative energy.

It is no accident that the whole course of events is encapsulated in a slogan lifted from the famous opening lines of the *Communist Manifesto*, a slogan modified by the demonstrators to make the capitalist spirit interchangeable with its former, "spectral" counterpart. Appearing on an electronic stock ticker displayed on the façade of an investment bank, it reads: "A SPECTER IS HAUNTING THE WORLD—THE SPECTER OF CAPITALISM" (96).

Security breakdown

This literary compilation of canonical formulae, drawn from both older and more recent analyses of capitalism—from Marx and Engels, through Schumpeter, up to Baudrillard, Boltanski, Chiapello, or Rifkin[2]—forms a tableau depicting the latest in a series of industrial revolutions. With the era of the steam engine and the regime of automation behind it, capitalism is now following a "digital imperative" and, in the process, seeking to regulate "every breath drawn by the billions of people who live on this planet" (24). This must be seen against the backdrop of the massive technological and economic upheaval brought about by the creation of electronic stock exchanges, the spread of computerized trading since the 1980s, the extension of networks, the introduction of ISDN, and the conversion of the frequency spectrum to 300 megahertz, all of which led to exponential growth in the mobility of capital transactions.

At the center of this euphoric alliance of information technology and finance capital, in DeLillo's novel, stands a course of events that lacks clear direction and follows a totally improbable and irrational course— and, in the process, yields an interpretation of what it means to live under conditions created by today's finance economy. This is revealed, on the one hand, by the way narrated events themselves unfold. For the path of DeLillo's allegory of capitalism leads further than expected. It not only runs from the eighty-ninth story of a luxury apartment tower to street-level shabby backyards; it not only moves from east to west, so following the prevailing direction of the American dream; and it not only draws a line from life to death, the place where exchange is no longer possible and all transactions cease. Like another modern Ulysses who spent an entire day wandering through a metropolis, the route taken by DeLillo's protagonist recalls the erratic itinerary of age-old voyages at sea. The allegory amounts in effect to a Homeric pastiche, recalling the fate of Odysseus in all its variants.

It is the path of the *nóstos*, the circuitous route of a long journey home. For DeLillo, however, the hero's homecoming has become a deadly descent into the realm of childhood, while the ship bearing the hero back from the Aegean is now an armored vehicle, cruising through dangerous metropolitan streets. Homer's Penelope, weaving as she waits, returns as a poetry-spinning heiress to billions. The hero falls into her arms not at the end of his journey but on the way, more than once and entirely by chance. Nausicaa, Circe, Calypso and the Sirens, oracles, and giants have assumed the form of female bodyguards, former lovers and eloquent scholars, as well as avant-garde artists, masked demonstrators and unemployed computer whizzes. And the circle of hell that Dante reserved for cunning Odysseus is realized, at the end of DeLillo's novel, in the sinister scenery of an endlessly drawn-out death moment.

Clearly, this epic tendency in the novel does not presuppose "a world already prosaically ordered," to borrow Hegel's definition of the modern novel. DeLillo leads us instead into a world in which events are loosely or merely episodically interlinked, appearing as external forces and hardships that ultimately take a turn for the worse as they interconnect and escalate in a fateful way. For Hegel, epic conventions are out of keeping with organized society, institutionalized community and above all the rule of law[4]; in DeLillo's hands they mark the entry-point into a zone of elemental danger. Whereas questions regarding security systems, preventive measures, risk assessment, surveillance and harm avoidance accumulate in thoroughly hyperbolical ways early on in the novel—"our system's secure" (12)—security increasingly breaks down as events unfold. The president of the United States, the last exponent of sovereign state power, now exists only as an image of one of the "undead" (77). If a particular moment can be said to represent this situation symbolically, it is the moment when the protagonist uses a code word to release the safety catch on his chief of security's automatic pistol and unexpectedly shoots him dead, thus turning this security measure against itself.

With that, DeLillo's allegory of capitalism steps—beyond the line—into a wilderness at the heart of civilization, a realm where terroristic impulses are given free rein, sudden assaults and attacks dictate the daily rhythm of life and barbarism is rife. It is the world of *hwa-byung, susto,* or *amok,* those culture-bound syndromes that have become bywords, in Korea, the Caribbean, or Malaysia, for the way indigenous people vent their repressed rage, pure horror, or panic in acts of uncontrolled violence.[5] The result is a caricature of an emotionally primitive landscape in which the excesses of the "fanatical tropics" (28) are mixed with the horrors of self-mutilation, slaughter, and "red meat" (14). DeLillo's protagonist is pursued in the end by the "power of pre-determined events" (147) and succumbs, as if to a "principle of fate" (107), to the death that has long awaited him. The word "speculator" derives from the Roman name for a sentry (*speculari*) who kept a lookout for danger or misfortune. In keeping with the general tendency of the narrative, it is this "seer" (46) who himself has taken on the role of the "dangerous person" by the end (19). Having become the point of attraction for all risky situations, he now lies there: robbed, abandoned, and exposed.

The unrepresentable

On the other hand, it is evident that this narrative interplay of archaic threat, excessive violence, and fatalism only repeats a framework of events dictated by the movements of global capital. Throughout his odyssey through the streets of Manhattan, the young fund manager speculates on the fall of the Japanese yen, thereby pursuing one of the most aggressive financial operations of all, the so-called carry trade. This form of credit-reliant takeover involves using borrowed capital to buy up shares of companies with healthy profit outlooks, as witnessed in recent years in the cases of Porsche/Volkswagen and Schaeffler/Continental. As the example of Packer Capital in DeLillo's novel indicates, this means that large quantities of potentially high-yielding shares can be bought with yen borrowed at low interest rates in expectation of a fall in the exchange rate of the yen, thus maximizing speculative gains. And something unprecedented and unexpected occurs as a result, providing the novel with one of its main plot devices. The erratic course that draws DeLillo's protagonist from one incident to another and on to his death is shadowed or doubled by a wild run on the currency market: "against expectations" (8), the Japanese yen climbs ever higher until nothing can stop its rise; Packer Capital's holdings are wiped out and its CEO is ruined—another odyssey with a fatal outcome.

In the end, DeLillo's novel leaves no doubt that something completely unthinkable and irrational has happened in this "yen-carry," something that is metastasizing "out of control" (85), follows no likely script, and no longer points to any plausible reality. The state of the world has become impossible to decipher. If the notorious "worldliness" of the modern and contemporary novel is bound up with the question of how events are ordered and by which rules, then DeLillo's novel registers a return to archaism in the most modern form imaginable; it leads us to suspect that the world of finance economics is battered by the storm winds of events signifying the gravest possible danger. Stock market transactions coupled with the fatality of brute force: here DeLillo is documenting a variation in a pattern of events that, a decade earlier, had been given the title *American Psycho*. Financial markets in a state of turmoil mirror zones of elemental danger. Together, they shape a narratological program that converts the dynamics of exchange rates into a pattern of epic fatefulness, making the advent of the unlikeliest outcome appear utterly inevitable.

"What is happening doesn't chart" (21): it cannot be represented. This trend in share prices is unrepresentable because it stages an "assault on the borders of perception" (21) by virtue of the inconceivably vast sums of money involved, awe-inspiring in their magnitude. It embodies an economic sublime that manifests itself without taking material form. To understand what this means, we need only recall that in 2000, for example, 1.9 billion dollars were flowing daily through the economic networks of New York City; or that even earlier, in the 1990s, fortnightly turnover there was already equivalent to worldwide economic output.[6] Beyond this, however, we are dealing here with what the traders call a "situation" (40), one of those improbable and rare events, unforeseeable and capricious, that appear without warning, like the actions of a "deranged killer" who for a long time lived undetected next door, posing as "an excellent citizen" and kindly "old neighbor."[7] This kind of event has also been described as a "black swan," meaning a unique occurrence with the following three attributes: first, it exceeds all expectations and indeed could never have been expected to take place; second, it has an extreme—in this case, fatal—impact; third, it provokes an obvious need for explanation, a retrospective search for coherence, background and plausibility. Just as the black swans of modern natural science appeared to be sheer impossibilities and could therefore become emblems of problematic inductive conclusions, so here they denote a leap that interrupts the linear sequence of events, leaving behind islands of turbulent activity that are scarcely credible, an excess of randomness.[8]

In any case, two things have happened by the end of this episodic course of events. On the one hand, disastrous speculative investment has destabilized the system itself and brought on a global crisis: "He knew it was the yen. His actions regarding the yen were causing storms of disorder. He was so leveraged, his firm's portfolio so large and sprawling, linked crucially to the affairs of so many key institutions, all reciprocally vulnerable, that the whole system was in danger" (116). In fact, the market of the new economic order did collapse in early 2000 for similar reasons. In the first two weeks of April that year, the NASDAQ, the US technology exchange, recorded a 27 percent price drop that analysts were at a loss to explain.[9] On the other hand, the manifest blindness of self-styled seers and speculators also had to be admitted: "I couldn't figure out the yen" (190). The world has become unreadable, its interconnections blurred. Things in general are running out of control. The series of stock exchange reports and currency events fits into no known pattern and progresses without apparent rationale. At the peak of the financial crisis of early 2000, DeLillo's protagonist finds himself in the same uncomfortable situation that Alan Greenspan, longtime director of the US Federal Reserve Bank and a staunch advocate of unregulated financial markets, was to confront eight years later. It was a situation in which he could no longer apply his "worldview," his "ideology," and long-held self-evident truths or interpretations. The "whole intellectual edifice" of the finance economy came crashing down.[10]

By tracing these erratic and apparently irrational movements, DeLillo's *Cosmopolis* naturally brings to mind the financial crises that followed each other in rapid succession from the twentieth century into the twenty-first: from the Wall Street crash of 1987 to the 1990 Japanese crisis, the bond market debacle of 1994, and the Russian collapse of 1998, followed by the so-called technology or dot-com bubble of 2000 and finally the disaster of 2007 to 2008 and beyond. Taken together, these were events that by all accounts of economic probability should never have occurred, or at most only once every several billion years. And DeLillo is perhaps also alluding to the surprising speculation on the exchange rate of the yen in relation to the US dollar during the 1990s, when the rise of the yen did appreciable and lasting damage to the Japanese economy, damage that would be repeated to ruinous effect between 1998 and 2000.[11]

Above all, however, the story centers quite obviously on one particular event, and a great deal is at stake in the way that event is presented: both the coherence of the narrated world and the rationality of the economic system. Here DeLillo is asking whether "plausible realities" that "can be traced and analyzed" will continue to exist (85); he explores the "techniques of charting" that enable us to grasp and "predict" the movements of money markets (75). The baffling fluctuation in the exchange rate of the yen, with all its calamitous effects, exemplifies the kind of unprecedented happening that now challenges all interpretative efforts, and it leads him to question nothing less than the sufficient reason behind it. What motivates such an event, what shapes its connections and makes it predictable, determining its possible or probable course? "The yen is making a statement. Read it!" (21). What kind of event is a current market valuation? What is expressed through it, how does it change, and what future course will it take? How necessary or fortuitous are the links between different events, and how erratically or sequentially are they made? Such questions lie at the heart of DeLillo's plot, but they are also the focal point for the will to knowledge of today's finance economy. DeLillo's literary text and the speculative play of signs it thematizes both pose a problem of interpretation. This is evidently related to the irruption of something unexpected and—to use one of Greenspan's phrases—to the dynamic of an "irrational exuberance" that puts the system of economic reason, or the rationality of this system, to the test.

Perplexity

All this inevitably points to a certain perplexity within economic science itself, prompting the open question: how, if at all, does an idea of the coherence of the economic universe manifest itself here? Economics—this dogma of our time—is in principle quite prepared to use completely different, contradictory interpretations to explain everything that happens in contemporary financial dealings, including crashes and crises. One of the most prominent of these interpretations is essentially orthodox in nature. It originates in the market fundamentalism of the Chicago school and calls itself the "efficient market hypothesis." According to this doctrine, financial markets represent the purest distillation of market activity in general. Unencumbered by transaction costs, unimpeded by transport needs and the difficulties of production, operated by rational, profit-oriented, and therefore reliable economic agents, they are the ideal, frictionless setting for price formation mechanisms and perfect competition. That is why prevailing prices and price fluctuations on these markets directly and exhaustively reflect all the available information. Under optimal conditions of market competition, so long as all players possess equal access to information relevant to pricing—for example, how much and how quickly they can buy—current price quotations will accurately convey the truth about economic activity in general at any given time. The assets to which these prices refer are never really under- or overvalued. Any errors and inefficiencies that may eventuate, such as major discrepancies between actual and forecast returns, are due only to various irritating impediments to free market activity and can quickly be rectified, given favorable conditions. As late as 2007, one of the founding fathers of this school of thought, Eugene Fama, considered it self-evident that there are no such things as "bubbles" in financial markets—the very idea is without foundation and makes no sense.[12] According to this view, all crises and depressions are nothing more than adjustment phases documenting the relentless forward march of economic reason. The market itself is what is real and hence rational.

There is another interpretation, which is a little less conservative but no less orthodox. Taking the most diverse financial crises as examples, it focuses on bubbles, runs, busts, and booms, speaking of "financial panic" or "euphoric escalations." Since the seventeenth century, and particularly since the nineteenth century, terms such as these have been used to address the sheer irrationality of speculative transactions that deviate fundamentally from all standard practices in the commodity market, from the principles of economic rationality, and from the basis of the so-called real economy. Daniel Defoe had already documented the susceptibility

of the "stock jobbers" to every kind of blindness and deception, show-
ing just how bottomless is the abyss into which totally irrational stock
market activity can lead. Somewhat later, examples of the influence of
mass hysteria, herd behavior, and blind imitation were identified in stock
market trade and speculation, ranging from Dutch tulip mania to the
English South Sea bubble or the French Mississippi bubble. Finally, the
high volatility of financial markets was cited as the reason for huge price
fluctuations that defied all rational expectations and for the highly aberrant, inefficient, and irregular ways in which the markets themselves operated.[13] Explanations such as these made it possible to assert the logical
inevitability of over- and undervaluation. Both could ultimately be traced
back to the influence of foreign, external, noneconomic factors: emotions,
for instance, or amateurish conduct, willful recklessness, extravagance,
greed, or sheer lack of common sense. Right up to the most recent collapse, financial markets and stock exchanges have been wrestling with a
real problem of inclusion. There are too many market players pursuing
all too incompetent operations or harboring sinister motives, triggering
irrational movements which, from time to time, give rise to exceptional
economic situations. Here then the market is neither efficient nor rational;
it is simply clueless.

Apart from an apparent consensus that price fluctuations on financial markets should be described as "turbulent currents" and "pure molecular flurries,"[14] there is not just disagreement among various schools of
thought here but flagrant disunity as to how one payment incident relates
to another and which forces of reason or unreason drive financial activity, provide its dynamics, and motivate its anomalies. This problematic is
further complicated by the question of what the play of economic signs
actually refers to. In other words, what do movements on the share market indicate? How are price fluctuations on stock exchanges and financial markets to be read and interpreted? What do they have the power to
represent?

This semiotic question in turn suggests a peculiar ambiguity in
finance economics. On the one hand, "fundamental analysis" concen-
trates on comparing price movements on financial markets with basal
economic data: with factors like productivity, returns, cost structures,
forecast dividends, discount rates, current accounts, or purchasing power.

Such factors provide a well-founded reference point for semiotic events and a realistic or objective orientation point for pricing. From this more or less classical perspective, finance prices and stock market quotations hover in the long term around the intrinsic value of companies or even whole national economies. Market trends and cycles would in this view be merely the more or less direct expression of a mute economic reality, which will ultimately assert itself thanks to its true and real underlying value.[15] A substantial frame of reference can thus be glimpsed beneath the fluctuations on currency and stock markets, with their shifting indices and quotations, and sufficient grounds for them can be found in the fundamental economic data.

On the other hand, the common practice of "technical analysis" operates with a form of observation that strictly disregards these referential dimensions. This is the mantic art practiced by banking and stock exchange personnel who, duly initiated into the mysteries of operations research and computational finance, glean prognostic clues for short-term investment decisions from the charts alone, that is, from their analysis of price movement characteristics. Their task is to register probable movements and so produce a composite image emerging from market hopes and expectations. As early as 1884, Charles Dow had calculated the daily average of a dozen of the most important share prices on Wall Street, using the data to create clear profiles of their movements and oscillation patterns at daily, monthly, yearly, and even longer intervals. His aim was to take a kind of barometric reading of the general business climate. Since the 1950s, at the latest, this approach has evolved into a successful business practice that decodes the meaning of recurring patterns and graphic samples to infer future probabilities from past quotations.

Better than all other data—the intrinsic or nominal value of shares, for example—these patterns supposedly reflect the true state of the market; they suggest the shape of things to come and confirm the expressive power of graphs to uncover hidden rhythms in the fluctuations of share market and currency transactions. Chartists and analysts speak here of "trend lines" and "trend channels," of "bear" and "bull models," of "inverted saucers," "head and shoulders top," "scallops," or "flags and pennants"—all characteristic formations that record trending directions and their turning points. These graphs do not purport to represent underlying value references. Instead, decisions about buying and selling are assessed solely by the way in which price signals interlink to form a pattern or syntagmatic chain. This results, on the one hand, in a kind of fair-hand or copybook version of the economic universe; in the trading rooms, signals from the outside world line up to form a noise-free tableau. On the other hand, it is in these same trading rooms that all the diverse species known to the world of finance meet and mingle. As in natural cycles, the market continually rehearses the same old motions and goes through the same routines. History itself becomes a form of endless recycling.[16]

From theodicy to oikodicy

These then are the standard models, positions, and procedures with which finance economics has endeavored, since the latter half of the twentieth century, to explain and represent the course and temporal dynamics of price formations on foreign exchange and stock markets. They all center on the enigma of price movements and fluctuations, as well as the related problems of timing and forecasting—and collectively, they bespeak a certain perplexity on the part of economics. The need for an explanation of financial activity calls for a comprehensive economic hermeneutics and reveals, above all, a chronic lack of unity in the various practical and theoretical formulae for intervention, the diagnoses and prescriptions offered by the discipline. All these interpretations and perspectives represent diverse and ultimately incompatible attempts to explain semiotic events situated at the center of modern finance economics. Not only do they draw attention to different levels or aspects of the same events; they emphasize different, partly contradictory, partly overlapping ideas about the coherence of the economic universe.

What is at stake here is nothing less than the logical consistency or orderliness of the financial system. What actually constitutes an event on financial markets? How does it (re)present itself? What brings it about and how does it fit in with other events situated on the same temporal axis? Which reality is expressed in the play of price signals and which underlying forces are at work in the modern financial market, setting trends and precipitating extraordinary events and crises? In the end, the controversy that rages on all these questions attests to the manifest insolubility of the questions themselves.

These are thus articles of dispute within the discipline of economic science. Whether or not lessons can be learned about future price flows and investments from the history of stock exchange movements; whether and how price fluctuations relate to fundamental economic data and conditions in the outside world; whether a fictitious play of signs has become detached from the so-called real economy, and if so, how this came about; whether movements on financial markets occur by necessity or by chance; to what extent sequences of monetary events are motivated or unfounded; whether the financial system functions efficiently or chaotically, or both at once; whether market dynamics represent rational interaction or the purest irrationality: all these questions reveal the models and hypotheses of finance economics to be action programs that take a historical and prognostic approach to the economic universe without reaching any consensus about what holds that universe together. Together, they lead us to the terrain of a dark and confused empiricism. They point to uncertainty about what economic reality actually is, and they hold a number of disappointments in store. "In no other field of empirical inquiry," the economist Wassily Leontief observed, "has such ingenious statistical machinery been utilized, and with such indifferent results."[17] The enigma of exceptional situations, rare events, and black swans remains.

At the vanishing point of finance-economic knowledge stands a problematic figure. The critical mass of events endlessly argued over by economists resembles a picture puzzle in which reason and unreason, order and chaos, a foreseeable course of world events and sheer unfettered contingency appear as indistinguishable. Questions, exegetical efforts, and controversies of this kind weigh all the more heavily since they bear on the validity of one of liberal economic theory's oldest and most deep-seated convictions: the conviction that market activity is an exemplary locus of order, integration mechanisms, harmonization, appropriate allocation, and hence social rationality, and that it demands to be represented in a coherent, systematic way. That is why it seems justified to identify, at the very heart of these disputes and in the explanatory attempts occasioned by financial crises, the reprise of a problematic that only older attempts to establish a theodicy had been compelled to address with comparable systematic rigor. Given that the capitalist economy has become our fate, given too our propensity to look to profit and economic growth to satisfy some remnant of the old hope for an earthly Providence, modern financial theory also cannot avoid confronting the baffling question of how, if at all, apparent irregularities and anomalies can exist in a system supposedly based on reason. In Leibniz's terms: Which events appear to be compatible (and hence "compossible") with which other events? Are relations between these events law-governed and if so, by which laws? And how can the existing economic world be "the best of all possible worlds"?

In any case, the questions that Kant used to test whether attempts at a theodicy were at all tenable would have to be directed, by analogy, to justifications of the current financial system. Here too it would be necessary to demonstrate that what seem to be "counterpurposive" and dysfunctional conditions are in fact nothing of the sort; or that they should not be judged as brute facts but as "the unavoidable consequence of the nature of things," as tolerable side effects of a generally satisfactory world order; or that they are to be ascribed, in the end, to the flawed nature of "beings in the world," the limited foresight of unreliable human actors.[18] Any such proof would require answers to the following questions: Are Greenspan's "irrational exuberances" really exceptional cases, or are they regular processes in the life of capitalist economies? Is the distinction between the rational and the irrational adequate to grasp the effects of this system? Are we really only dealing with the unreliability and limited insight of finance professionals? Or is economic rationality directly confronting its own irrationality here? Can a form of order be discerned here or merely a haphazard aggregate of disparate individual actions? Does the system in fact work rationally and efficiently? And is there any plausible narrative for events in the finance economy?

Just as the Lisbon earthquake of 1755 once shook modern theodicy to its foundations, so the financial tremors of the last twenty years threaten to undermine the scientific status of economic theory. What is at issue is nothing less than the validity, possibility, and tenability of a liberal or capitalist *oikodicy*,[19] a theodicy of the economic universe: the inner consistency of an economic doctrine that—rightly or wrongly, for good or ill—views contradictions, adverse effects, and breakdowns in the system as eminently compatible with its sound institutional arrangement.

Idyll of the Market I

Social physics

What comes into question with this oikodicy is one of the founding ideas of political economy. According to its assumptions, only the market and its players can guarantee spontaneous order, systematic organization, and the workings of Providence in the world. The history of political economy is the history of this optimistic conception. Originating in seventeenth-century natural law, political advice literature, and moral philosophy, economic science achieves systematic consistency in the expectation that, following on from advances in mathematics, astronomy, physics, and medicine, laws of motion analogous to those governing the stars and natural bodies could be discovered in human actions as well. The formulation of general laws for the movement of natural bodies—from the astronomy of Copernicus to the physics of Galileo and Newton—accords with the idea that there is a specific rationality to be found in political and social life once it has detached itself from the exemplary model of divine world government to seek its principles in itself. By the eighteenth century, ever more urgent calls for a Leibniz, a Descartes, or a Newton of politics and society were voiced: for someone who would systematize the study of social and political dynamics in the same way these illustrious predecessors had systematized the empirical study of nature. When it was claimed, for example, that the rules of geometry apply just as much in society as they do in nature, or that the law of gravity is no less valid in the moral than in the physical universe, these were no mere analogies. Rather, they amounted to the claim that the structure of social order can only be legitimated through the empirical investigation of its mechanisms, forces, and elements.

Early Modern debates about reason and natural law had already unfolded on the basis of a political epistemology that posited a coherent and self-perpetuating order behind disparate individual phenomena, as well as law-governed relations between apparently unconnected movements, things, and beings. That is why recourse was so often taken to the systemic concepts of astronomy, which provided a model for law-governed processes and changes, for relations between forces and movements. It is also why attempts were made to develop a politics based on physics or mechanics, discovering a hidden interplay of forces behind modes of social interaction. And finally, it is why thinkers sought a definition of human "nature" as both the agent of these dynamics and their most problematic example. In Hobbes's words:

as in a watch or some such small engine, the matter, the figure and motion of the wheels, cannot well be known except it be taken in sunder, and viewed in parts; so to make a more curious search into the rights of States and duties of Subjects, it is necessary (I say not to take them in sunder, but yet that) they be so considered as if they were dissolved (i.e.) that we rightly understand what the quality of human nature is, in what matter it is, in what not fit to make up a civil government, and how men must be agreed among themselves, that intend to grow up into a well-rounded State.[1]

If, then, in modern times the earth not only begins to rotate around the sun but money too starts to rotate around the earth,[2] these revolutions are evidently complemented by an anthropological one, which no longer presents a mere "image" of mankind but mankind as it "really" is—and this redefinition becomes the starting point for new conceptions of sociopolitical order. At any rate, ever since the Baroque, teachers of natural law and moral philosophers have generally agreed that human beings are no longer to be understood simply as *zoa politika*, as political animals who are directly and instinctively adapted to life in society. In contrast to most other creatures, human beings have instead shown themselves to be dysfunctional and quite unsuited to communal existence. By nature, they are disagreeable companions for their fellows—and an extensive literature about such concepts as "self-love" or "self-preservation" proves that here, so far as human beings are concerned, we can only join Kant in speaking of "unsociable sociability" or a "nation of devils." According to this view, "real" human beings find themselves in a hopelessly "ruined state"; they are "creatures filled with all kinds of wicked cravings."[3] The central focus for political empiricism is now a specimen of the human race whose unreliable impressions and illusions, twisted passions and desires, must all be taken into account. It is possible to see, in reflections of this kind, the emergence of a political anthropology, perhaps even the genesis of the anthropological question itself. Above all, however, they constitute an essential step toward grasping and realizing new ways of conceiving the mechanisms of social interaction. The identification of a new type of human being thus coincides with novel conceptions of social order, conceptions in which market events and political economy will ultimately assume a privileged role. How is this to be understood? How does this human being, who is equally real and corrupt, differ from the old Adam of Christian theology? And what is the modern oikodicy based on?

Private vices . . .

It first needs to be emphasized that human beings of this type—as they are described from around the seventeenth century onwards—are the creatures of their desires; they are moved by appetite and aversion, attraction and repulsion, and hence are constitutionally defined by their social deficits and malfunctions. That is not the whole story, however. For it was now claimed that, contrary to expectations, these very deficiencies were what made it possible for a social order to emerge that works better, perhaps, than any other. This is what was meant by the famous formula: "private vices, public benefits." The phrase was first used in Bernard Mandeville's early-eighteenth-century work of moral philosophy, *The Fable of the Bees*, and went on to enjoy such great success that it gave rise to a comprehensive social theorem. As Mandeville saw it, human beings are by nature dominated and their hearts inflamed by affects, desires, and passions, including even such formerly deadly sins as *superbia, avaritia, invidia, luxuria*, that is, pride, avarice, envy, and gluttony. All the same— so Mandeville's argument goes on—it is not the moderate tendencies but precisely the immoderate ones that are genuinely creative, cunning, and productive; furthermore, all these various passions incite and agitate each other in such a way that they ultimately balance each other out and compensate for each other's ill effects. Thus one man's avarice holds another's "prodigality" in check, so that through their scheming and cunning they both contribute to the common good.

That is the central point of the argument: what in individuals appears sinful, irregular, and reprehensible gives rise, in the big picture, to a dynamic and harmonious order. As Mandeville writes, a good statesman only has to reckon with the worst in his subjects; he has no need to take virtues and moderating qualities into account, only the extremes of unbridled passion. He observes their vices acting like a reagent, combining and reacting with each other; he sees how "both melt away alike, and they consume themselves by being beneficial to the several compositions they belong to."[4] Modern humans come into the world not merely as rational beings but as particularly passionate subjects who can transform even the old Christian deadly sins into new social assets.

Precisely because human beings are asocial—this is how the surprising argument goes—they help contribute to social order; precisely because they are unreliable, they can be integrated into society as reliable, known quantities. How is this possible? By what mechanism can lawfulness be produced from anomic beings? What dynamic is at play here and what is its overall function in the system? Here too the answers given by the English empiricists, French moralists, and German social engineers coincide in one essential point: all these affective dynamics come together in the mechanism of self-interest. At the heart of all (mis)deeds and passions, all desires and inclinations, lies an irreducible element which, since the seventeenth century, has gone by the name of "interest" or "self-interest." The concept of (self-)interest probably originated in raison d'état or national interest before passing into social theory—and the aspects that enabled it to become a theoretical and practical cornerstone for the order of modern commercial relations will be sketched in very general terms below.[5]

Interests

In the first place, interest is to be understood as a final, indissoluble atom of social relations: all behavior, even the most apparently disinterested, is ultimately motivated by self-interest. Whatever someone wants or desires, wherever inclination or passion drives him—in any more or less conscious decision-making process the logic of preference is at work and it always culminates in what is best for oneself. Even the vilest cravings and most heated passions are stabilized by a trace element of self-interest that dictates the choice of the more pleasant, less painful option. Self-interest thus proves to be a form of volition that works not through asceticism, self-mastery, and restraint but, on the contrary, through self-assertion. Self-interest does not countenance self-denial. It functions as an unprincipled principle. It is realized in concrete situations, in the face of concrete alternatives; it knows no universal (moral) laws and reacts to the chance nature of world events. Interested subjects are therefore anything but moral or legal subjects; they refuse to be denied. Crucially, however, those who act out of self-interest have no alternative but to cooperate with others in trade and exchange. In communicating their inclinations, they create the ground rules for social engagement. It is in self-interest that the inclinations and passions of all parties meet, and it is precisely in their pursuit of that interest that the social and political laws of nature are revealed. Just as natural bodies succumb to the law of gravity, so society is determined by the law of self-interest. Therein lies the analogy between physics and human interactions: the laws of cosmology dictate the government of society. As the French moral philosopher Helvetius put it, "If the physical universe is subject to the laws of motion, the moral universe is no less subject to those of interest."[6]

Taken together, all these changes add up to nothing short of a moral and anthropological revolution. The image of mankind formed in the seventeenth and eighteenth centuries is one unblemished by original sin. Human beings are neither good nor evil, neither devilish nor angelic, but functional and dysfunctional at one and the same time. They are dysfunctional because they participate in society only reluctantly and by chance; and they are functional because this very reluctance ensures that everyone's self-interested pursuit of his own desires and aspirations results in a lawful and predictable whole. This is *the* law of society, and it makes for better government than all other moral precepts or legal rules. An older wisdom that perceived public loss in private gain and demanded that limits be set on private interest "so that your neighbor too may live"[7] is thus inverted and transformed into a system of fruitful opportunism.

Since the seventeenth century, then, deep within the human breast a heart has been beating that burns with desire; all desires and passions, however, only serve to mask a naked, irreducible element of sheer self-interest. This is what drives social interactions, producing order out of disorder and lawfulness out of lawlessness. Even today there are those who continue to identify in this process a mechanism for transforming sporadic isolated actions into predictable and orderly sequences. In his critique of the behavioral foundations of economic theory, for example, Amartya Sen remarks: "It is possible to define the interest of a person in such a way that in every single decision they make they are seen to be following their own interests."[8] At the same time, self-interest became the motivating force of a new, "realistic" type of human being, who now had to be redefined as *homo economicus*. His various passions and interests provide the mechanism by which social reality is produced in the first place. As a result, a systematic web of interrelations arises, natural law is installed in the midst of society, and a particular system of human interactions is privileged that is finally realized in the market economy. The way of thinking about markets and economic systems that took shape from the seventeenth century onward relates not only to relations between prices, commodities, and payments, but also to the domain governed by the law of self-interest, and therefore to the essentially economic substrate of human nature. This substrate is the medium by which an elementary form of social reality directly reproduces itself, a medium that connects stimuli with responses and responses with communications. This leads to a further question in the present context: what makes for the efficiency of *homo economicus*? How exactly does he navigate these systems? What concrete form does his law-governed activity take? And what role does he assume in a new oikodicy?

This new human type, driven by self-interest, moves so confidently in an inscrutable world because he himself is blind and limited, sees everything with the "foolish mole-like eyes of egotism,"[9] and does not aspire to any kind of overview. He operates like a tiny island of rationality in an entirely contingent and irrational world. Like one of his most illustrious models, Robinson Crusoe, marooned on his desert island, he knows that order in the world is neither preestablished nor impossible but must be wrested into being. *Homo economicus* specializes in making fresh starts and coping with difficult situations; he is able to do so because he categorizes things in the world, not according to whether they are good or bad, true or false, just or unjust, but by the criteria of profit and loss. To this day, economic theory has testified to this truth: there would be no "economic" human beings if reality did not afford an opportunity for organizing the multiplicity of its phenomena and signals in a hard-headed, business-like way, according to the advantages and disadvantages they present. Those who follow their own inclinations and interests insist on the limited nature of those inclinations and interests. Furthermore, they single-mindedly disregard the rest of the world, assuming at best that everyone else shares their own narrow-mindedness, which transforms passions into interests and interests into advantages. Their rationality is rational only because it remains undemanding and local. As a subject, *homo economicus* would therefore be constrained by his limited knowledge; failing to see the sequence of causes and effects, he would himself produce effects that he does not recognize, does not intend, and which escape his blinkered perspective.

Invisible hands

It is, however, precisely these unintended effects, originating from limited interests and selfish tendencies, which cannot help turning out to the good of the whole. This turn became a commonplace of bourgeois moral philosophy in the eighteenth century; by furthering talk of a "harmony of interests," it created the expectation of an earthly Providence.[10] It is exemplified, above all, by an image that gained notoriety, at least with Adam Smith, as the "invisible hand," an image which to this day still illustrates the assumptions made by political economy about order in the world. The famous reference from *The Wealth of Nations* (1776), the second book in a lecture course on moral philosophy, reads as follows:

He [the economic agent] generally neither intends to promote the public interest, nor knows how much he is promoting it. By preferring the support of domestic to that of foreign industry, he intends only his own security; and by directing that industry in such a manner as its produce may be of the greatest value, he intends only his own gain. And he is in this, as in many other cases, led by an invisible hand to promote an end which was no part of his intention. By pursuing his own interests he frequently promotes that of the society more effectually than when he really intends to promote it. I have never known much good done by those who affected to trade for the public good.

Transparent nontransparency thus prevails here. On the one hand, there is evidently some quasi-divine point from which the workings of the whole system appear fully transparent. On the other hand, the system only works if no agent occupies this position. The satisfaction of needs—and hence social reciprocity—does not depend on the goodwill of the individual, whether it be the butcher, the baker, or the candlestick maker, but rather on the fact that individuals are perpetually in conflict, "perceiv[ing] their own interests" only and looking out for their own advantage. Social order is not built on oversight, charity, and cooperativeness. When it comes to communicating our interests, it is much more a matter of "negotiating, exchanging and purchasing"; in trade, self-interest ultimately discovers the principle of social reason.[11]

This brings us to one of the most important components of the new social law and the oikodicy, a defining feature of *homo economicus* and his milieu, the market. Economic beings are reliable on account of their very limitations, they are social due to their lack of sociality, and it is only through their self-interested participation in trade that they can be brought to serve a purpose extrinsic to themselves. Above all, they best exercise control over themselves and others if they are left uncontrolled. There is nothing—and this will be one of the leitmotifs of the liberalism to come—more harmful than a government that wants to do good. On the contrary, what is called for here is a Mephistophelian agenda, one that takes its cue from a power "which would do evil constantly and constantly does good," inadvertently producing what is best for all. Civil society, which constitutes itself as the milieu of *homo economicus*, is governed by the principle of nontransparency or inscrutability; there is no benevolent political actor, possessed of an all-encompassing overview and piercing insight, who might be willing and able to do what is good for everyone. And it is precisely the blindness of self-seeking interests, rather than any clarity or broadness of vision, which guarantees the pursuit of a universal goal. That is what it means to say that *homo economicus* is the subject of his limited interests but the medium of civil society.

Although Adam Smith was responsible for coining one of the most popular slogans for describing how a market economy operates, its semantics are determined by two further aspects. On the one hand, if we follow the tangled history of the "invisible hand" metaphor, we can see how through this metaphor theological and cosmological questions were deposited in the field of social ontology. A century before Adam Smith, for instance, the metaphor referred to something secretly at work in relations between natural things, a cosmological phenomenon that, like the mechanism of a clock, hides behind the clearly visible hands and dial: "For *Nature* works by an *Invisible Hand* in all things."[12] The *manus gubernatoris* of Scholastic philosophy, the guiding hand of God invisibly directing all Creation, returns as an influential theological metaphor for the Providence manifest in the natural order, the *oeconomia naturae*. And before the "invisible hand" appeared in *Wealth of Nations* as a topos for the law-governed activity that turns self-interest and the striving for gain to the general good, this expression occurred in Smith himself in an entirely different yet equally significant context.

In his *History of Astronomy*, probably written around 1758, not only did Smith attempt an apologia for the Newtonian world system, with its laws of gravity and inertia; he also casually remarked on the inability of polytheistic religions to trace irregular events in the natural world—events in which they saw the miraculous power of the ancient gods at work—back to regularly occurring patterns. While it is only natural that "fire burns and water refreshes," or that "heavy bodies descend and lighter substances fly upward," extraordinary phenomena such as lightning, thunder, or storms call for explanation—and for this the ancients would in the end simply turn to Jupiter's "invisible hand."[13] Here too the invisible hand is treated as a cosmological fact; and just as an invisible hand will later bring the unpredictable inclinations of self-seeking subjects to order, so too here an invisible hand shows how irregular natural events manifest the workings of divinely ordained laws. As a result of such supernatural intervention, earthly matters are brought into conformity with Providence, irregularities are translated into order, and diffuse forces and movements are made to bear witness to an invisible power linking them together. All this activity by invisible hands indicates that hidden manipulations—in the most literal sense—intervene both in the natural course of events and in the dynamics of social interaction.

On the other hand, it should not be forgotten that Smith presented another version of his concept of the "invisible hand" in the first volume of his 1759 essay on moral philosophy, *The Theory of Moral Sentiments*. And here *homo economicus* is defined by more than his failure to see the whole situation, his lack of a comprehensive overview. Economic beings can only function to the extent that they are always missing something even more fundamental. In Smith's words, the "proud and unfeeling landlord" may let his gaze wander over his vast fields and in his imagination consume the entire harvest without even sparing a thought for "the wants of his brethren." The "capacity of his stomach," however, "bears no proportion to the insatiability of his desires," functioning instead as a physical or rather physiological limit. That is why he must distribute the rest of his harvest whether he wants to or not, and it is also why it is precisely through his desire for more "luxuries," "baubles and trinkets" that he satisfies the needs of others. Despite or precisely because of their "natural selfishness and rapacity," the rich share their wealth with the poor. In Smith's words, this means that

they are led by an invisible hand to make nearly the same distribution of the necessaries of life, which would have been made, had the earth been divided into equal portions among all its inhabitants; and thus without intending, without knowing it, advance the interest of the society and afford the means for the multiplication of the species.[14]

Here too the drive to satisfy blind egoistic impulses advances the general good. Furthermore, Smith introduces a permanently insatiable desire, one that is more or less unlimited, goes beyond needs and their satisfaction, and even exceeds the capacity of the body containing it. Marx was later to call this the "addiction to abstract pleasure," displayed by capitalists, whose drive to accumulate money and capital stands out of all proportion to any real concrete need. And this is a further characteristic both of economic beings and the economic system they propel. For the basic components of this system are not simply commodities or necessities but object relations, preferences, wishes, and desires—and it is precisely their immoderate nature that guarantees a modicum of balance in the system overall. Since the end of the eighteenth century, at the latest, economic subjects have been produced by internalizing what they lack; they have become automata of desire who must necessarily want what they do not receive. Like Goethe's Faust, *homo economicus* is someone who feels the pang of emptiness in plenitude, discovers what he wishes for when he misses out on it, and ultimately masters the art of insufficiency—the art, that is, of searching in infinite striving for finite and always scarce commodities) This is the "desiring-machine" (Deleuze/Guattari) of *homo economicus*, who with his egoistic preferences, unintended consequences, limited knowledge, and limitless desires wants what he cannot do and does what he cannot want.

Homo economicus

Since the seventeenth century—to put it briefly—the discourses of natural rights and moral philosophy have provided some of the building blocks for an all-purpose definition of *homo economicus*. These discourses connect assumptions about the state of the world with presuppositions about human nature, and they have led to a long-lasting, radical change in the moral household and in the economy of human interrelations. This means, first, that modern *homo economicus* appears on the scene not merely as a rational subject but also as a passionate one, whereby these passions are regulated via a mechanism of interests. Second, he acts as a blind subject with limited knowledge. It is precisely through this blindness that he produces—unintentionally and unconsciously—harmonious social relations. For this reason, he follows a specific path in life. *Homo economicus* acquires wisdom through his ignorance and gets ahead in life thanks to his limited awareness and narrow horizons. Incidentally, a similar contradiction can be found in the plot structure of the German *Bildungsroman*: Wilhelm Meister, too, arrives at his rightful place in life precisely through his limited knowledge and the unintended consequences of his actions, as if steered there by an invisible, "higher hand."[15] Third, *homo economicus* is an enemy of the state in a special sense. As far as he is concerned, the implementation of a good system—involving laws, institutions, administration, and so on—conflicts with the good implementation of systematicity itself. With his appearance in the sphere of a liberal economy from the late eighteenth century onwards, an obstacle or "bane of excessive government" is now discerned and the mechanism of the market becomes the test for the efficiency of all the "artificial arrangements" that shape the life of "civil society."[16] And fourth, this hostility to government interference does not detract, as might be expected, from *homo economicus* developing into an eminently governable character type. The priority given to economics, trade, and market forces creates a milieu in which the desires and interests of *homo economicus* regulate and control themselves, balancing and offsetting each other in the process. The law that establishes order here is not external to individual players. It arises from their selfish hearts and governs them better and more effectively than any ruler; it acts, in short, as an invisible hand. *Homo economicus*—this will be his constantly repeated claim—no longer needs either the wise lawmaker or the prudent politician. Civil society, which has been created by his agency, gives itself over to a dynamic in which the players, for all that they may behave erratically and idiosyncratically as individuals, are nonetheless predictable and calculable as a collective and can therefore be expected to conduct themselves in accordance with legal statutes and moral principles. For this reason, the market is not just one forum among others but the site of social order as such: a catalyst that, in transforming passions into interests and selfish interests into amicable concord, directly follows a law of nature. The various evils—and in this we hear the echoes of an older theodicy— are more than just a necessary part of the system; they are what justifies its harmonious mode of operation.

All these elements define the domain of *homo economicus* and form a liberal idyll of the market that inspired characteristic Enlightenment praise of the "sweet" and "gentle" spirit of trade,[17] but also sends more recent representatives of the discipline of economics into raptures. Milton Friedman, for one, maintained that we have the miracle of the free market to thank for the fact that prices arising from voluntary transactions between buyers and sellers actually coordinate the activities of millions of market participants. The price system takes over the task of replacing an absent center and guarantees that social order emerges, as unconsciously as it does unintentionally, from divergent individual forces. Without having to love each other, indeed without really even having knowingly to cooperate with each other, we all work towards the common good by pursuing our own self-interest. Under the aegis of that ominous invisible hand, our sole responsibility as economic agents is to be responsible for nothing and nobody but ourselves.[18]

Naturalism

Put somewhat crudely, we would have to speak here of the emergence of a liberal despotism. A market of this kind not only demands a certain amount of effort to free its subjects to pursue their own desires and interests. The expansion of local markets into a market society also requires that the relationship between economics, politics, and society be recalibrated. The market is charged with executing a law of nature, as it were, and all other laws and institutions are to be assessed by the way they ensure compliance with this natural law, thereby guaranteeing the spontaneous operation of economic mechanisms. In this respect the market has become an arena for the realization of practical reason.

This momentous moral-philosophical shift was probably first made explicit by the physiocrats, the politico-economic theorists to whom the earliest attempts at a systematic account of economic life may be attributed. For this was precisely what the physiocrats had in mind when they talked of a *despotisme légal*. Whereas the order of nature (*ordre de la nature*) defines the rules of economic exchange and in so doing follows the dictates of an immutable natural law, the task of the moral order (*ordre naturel*) is to make all market participants duty-bound to act on guidelines that comply with the principle of this natural law. This results in a "jurisprudence of mankind," a *jus publicum universale* that aligns institutions, legal principles, and rules of behavior with natural processes and discovers the site of their conformity in market mechanisms. The market guarantees that natural laws can pertain equally to moral life; and the forces of the market make it possible for economic law, in particular, to represent natural rights in general.[19] One inevitable consequence of this overall accommodation to the market is that the distinction, stemming from the modern theory of the state, between civil society and the state of nature no longer makes sense. The market cancels or elides this distinction and eliminates the associated aporias of natural law. It circumvents the social contract and presents itself as a kind of civil *état de nature*.

[What later goes by the name of "liberalism" thus first took the form of naturalism, which defined so-called market freedoms primarily in terms of a duty and an obligation: the duty to relinquish control of economic subjects and a corresponding obligation to subordinate governments and their agents to primordial market laws. This naturalism of governance[20] applies the principles of natural law to institutions and thereby lays claim to a moral-philosophical justification for liberal economics, but it is really built on theoretical foundations that secure the legal force of economic life in the first place. For the market becomes the gold standard of economic and social legitimacy only on condition that it provides a paradigmatic example of balance and equilibrium. In the context of protracted debates about the allocation of grains and foodstuffs, this means that reflections on the market have been determined, since the middle of the eighteenth century, by the question of the relationship between the system of needs and the corresponding supply situation. The movements of the market are dictated by the dynamics of prices. Here, in the relation between supply and demand, we discover the mysterious "equilibrium of the whole"; here too, in the process of price formation on free markets, we discover the hand of Providence working with "boundless love" to turn human commerce and all the desires circulating through it to the common good. The benevolent work of nature recurs in the balance and equilibrium of trade.[21]

System of prices

Thus exchange, or more precisely the buyer-seller relationship, becomes the basis of all social relations, so inaugurating political economy's love affair with Robinsonades: take three islands, one of which produces only crops, the second only wool, and the third only wine. The surpluses of one island answer to the needs of the other two; and where surplus products are exchanged for necessities, not only is the insularity of each island cancelled out but a balance is struck between two desires, which are equalized and harmonized in a fair, appropriate or "natural" price. In essence, this is why the circulation of commodities and money was pictured as a system of communicating vessels, in which ongoing exchange operations cause surpluses to flow where they will be most useful and necessary and where they can continue guaranteeing the balance of the whole.[22] In this respect, too, Adam Smith was to offer a systematic account, formulating a price theory that still provides inspiration today for its "beauty" and for representing the first achievement of a "free economic order."[23]

Smith's equilibrium theory is determined by the fortuitous correlation between two interacting price types: on the one hand, the actual market prices, which result from the fluctuating proportions of supply and demand; on the other, the intrinsic, central, or "natural price," calculated by factoring in expenditure on ground rent, wages, and capital gain. And this goes to show the beneficence of the system: the "interest" of all "laborers," "dealers," and "landlords" always works to ensure that the "natural price" is, so to speak, the central point toward which "the prices of all commodities are continually gravitating. Different accidents may sometimes keep them suspended a good deal above it, and sometimes force them down even somewhat below it. But whatever may be the obstacles which hinder them from settling in this center of repose and continuance, they are constantly tending towards it."[24] Even if sudden and apparently inexplicable price fluctuations should cause anxiety, even if monopolies, state interventions, or privileges may obstruct or falsify the play of market forces, economic science has a soothing explanation to hand: just as heavenly bodies periodically rotate around a stable orbit, according to the analytic mechanics of Lagrange or Laplace, so market prices, which are more or less a matter of chance, likewise oscillate in the long term around a natural price and find a rational basis in this price. With that, not only do they provide the optimal distribution of all resources; they also make it possible for entire national economies to strive towards a state of equilibrium. The market solves a problem of justice and distributes wealth in appropriate portions. There may be little agreement about the actual status to be accorded this equilibrium in the nascent discipline of political economy (for example, about whether it should be understood as an optimum, a principle, or a reality), and Smith himself may never have set out exactly what he understood by equilibrium; nonetheless, equilibrium theory became a crucial element of economic knowledge and was passed on through Ricardo, Walras, Jevons, and Pareto to the doctrines of the twentieth century.[25] Economic theory was born as a theory of equilibrium.

A kind of theoretical wish fulfillment was thus formulated with regard to market mechanisms. The question of the laws governing social interactions leads from blind passions and selfish interests to the question of balance and equilibrium. Such equilibrium is only guaranteed, however, by a market in which disparate tendencies, forces, and interests are coordinated, moderated, and harmonized by the system of prices. The dynamic of price formation thus not only presents an analogy to the cosmic order, in which gravitational forces ensure the evenness of eternal heavenly orbits despite all their apparent irregularities. It also provides sufficient grounds for social order to be possible in the first place. The market is both the means and the end of organized social relations. This model of market activity was to have a great future. In this model, the mechanisms of human interaction take after the processes of economic life, while these processes in turn function in line with market forces and price movements. According to such a view, it is the market that translates spontaneous, isolated actions into orderly consequences. It is the market that establishes a satisfactory relationship between demand and production costs, allowing prices to gravitate towards the natural or true worth of the products traded; and market forces are ultimately what guarantee the optimal allocation of resources, commodities, and wealth. Finally, since Adam Smith, economists have believed it is the mechanism of the market that transforms the disparate activities and interests, the willful behavior of its players, into a rational or law-governed set of relationships, thereby setting it on a providential course. Where global conditions have become inscrutable, human beings deficient, and their fates obscure, the market has apparently created a limited yet impregnable preserve of bourgeois order. From the eighteenth century right up to the present, the theory of free markets has thus set about crediting market processes with an exemplary capacity for maintaining order, thereby establishing a standard that, better than any other model, can serve as a measure of harmonious social order.

Interpersonal relations are rationalized in trade and the exchange of goods, but it is precisely for this reason that the market and the price system are more than just a matter of economics. Little as Adam Smith should retrospectively be held to account for offering an unabashed apologia for emerging capitalism or for reducing social life to purely economic activity, it is thanks to him that economic processes were seen as foundational to society and the market understood as the instrument of a spontaneous social order. The "economic ideology" was formed not on the periphery of modern social thought but at its center. The idea of the market attests to its origins in moral philosophy and occupies the place of a practical truth in the scientific study of politics, society, and history.[26] In the apotheosis of this idea, the laws of social interaction have been naturalized. What since the eighteenth century has been called civil society was founded in the idyll of the market and stands or falls with this oikodicy.

3

The Time of Capital

Equilibrium

The ideas of balance and equilibrium are viewed to this day as the most important contribution of economic science to a general understanding of social processes. An oikodicy has formed around these key economic principles, a liberal idyll of the market that offers a kind of fable about the evolution of market society. This oikodicy describes how scattered market players, keen to trade and motivated by self-interest, react to price signals and seek each other out in the marketplace. In doing so, they act on the assumption that market laws and mechanisms make for an exemplary form of distributive justice, as well as providing a basis for social order and an efficient instrument for the implementation of practical reason. The liberal discourse of political economy does something even more remarkable, however. It opens up new perspectives in social ontology by drawing together certain traditional lines of thought and presuppositions, including the anthropological substrate of *homo economicus*, cosmological ideas of systematic functioning, and various physico-theological rudiments.

Since Adam Smith, at the latest, hypothetical notions of "balance" have been an essential prerequisite for the reconception of society as "market society." We speak of balance between divergent interests, between buyers and sellers, between supply and demand, between quantities of goods and money, and between natural or "intrinsic" values and market or "exchange" prices. Even if the concept of equilibrium has taken different theoretical and epistemological forms on its journey from classical economics, via the marginalists of the nineteenth century, to twentieth-century neoliberalism, these versions share a limited spectrum of basic assumptions. They assume that all market players are interested in maximizing profit or use-value, that a self-regulating relationship between different quantities, forces, and other factors obtains, that exchange mechanisms operate most effectively when arbitrary intrusions and interventions are kept to a bare minimum, and hence that the market should be seen as an exemplary arena for the clarification of otherwise inscrutable and opaque forms of social interaction.[1] Whether market equilibrium is understood as trivial, mechanical, and deterministic or seen rather to result from a complex system of dynamic forces, it is by reference to this idea that the market becomes a fundamental social institution, and indeed that society constitutes itself in the first place.

That also affects the distinctive character of political economy, together with its status as a discourse and as a theoretical practice. On the one hand, this means that economic theory itself adheres to a principle of economy: it trusts in Ockham's razor, reduces complexity, relies on neat models and effective simplifications, and in general accepts that the world is simpler than we think it is. The adoption of idealized, decentralized models of the market, which reduce the opacity of commercial interrelations to the competitive reactions of rational agents, is indispensable if one wants to operate with coherent economic systems in a coherent way. Political economy always has a range of robust theories to offer. On the other hand, however, those who operate with such theories do not apply them naively. For it is by no means certain that fully decentralized markets actually exist—markets, that is, that are motivated by self-interest, guided by price signals, and guarantee a perfect distribution of economic resources. The less such abstractions apply to the confused situations that prevail in the real world, the greater is the intellectual onus on political economy to demonstrate that even if there are no such things as ideal markets they nonetheless *could* exist. In other words, while the assumptions behind such markets may not be "realistic," they do at least stand a chance of being realized.[2] It may be possible to detect the workings of a social imaginary in all this, by which we mean those efficacious fictions which inform the self-understanding of societies, coordinate social and symbolic practices, and provide intuitively justified images or self-evident truths to determine how society functions and which options for action are available at any given time. Accordingly, the fiction of self-balancing market forces provides a privileged source of images from which modern societies draw their self-representations.[3]

What this conception provides above all, however, is the lasting core of a liberal oikodicy: it ensures the integrity of a possible world. It justifies itself not simply by reference to what is, but to what might yet be realized. However pragmatic or visionary political economy may have been since its emergence in the eighteenth century, it has clearly never constituted itself by simply documenting the developments and processes of actual economic events. The concept of the market took shape *before* the market began to function. Although political economy is at pains to insist that it transcribes real-world relations, this reality is still seen as unfulfilled, as an all too incoherent and incomplete process. Its realism is prospective; it is always anticipating a virtual reality which it projects into objects and relations. That is the distinguishing feature of the dual structure of modern economic science or, if we can put it this way, its performative force: the concept of the market is at once a model *and* a "truth program" (Foucault). It is thus fully invested in the challenge of making the laws of the market themselves come true. Facts and events are interpreted in terms of how they fit into this project; reality is defined in terms of what can be realized. Modern political economy thus focuses primarily on the question of how the possible world of the market—and hence history itself—is a priori feasible. This question can be restated with Kant's philosophical-historical irony: as far as the project of political economy is concerned, it can be said that here "the prophet himself occasions and produces the events he predicts."[4]

Competition

This has two consequences, which shape the themes of modern political economy and define its discourse. First, from the nineteenth century (if not earlier), the idea of competition is assigned a crucial logical and strategic position in arguments about market activity. According to a programmatic essay written by Friedrich Hayek in 1968, the distinctive methodological feature of competition theory is that it can only prove its worth in the first place by denying all need for empirical verification. To the extent that competition and rivalry mean that agents in ill-defined situations act in unexpected ways to produce unpredictable outcomes, the concept of competition only makes sense if it is not tested on individual empirical cases. It thus presupposes the constitutive openness of competitive processes. Nobody knows who will win or lose in a competitive situation, or how, where, and when something will be won or lost, or what that will be. All that can be verified is that competitive societies distribute opportunities for competition more efficiently than other social systems. This means that an economic theory of competition cannot make definitive statements about the future of particular events and allocations, only statements about the kinds of structure and patterns of order that arise from competition.

Competition makes pattern prediction possible. This is due not least to the good fortune that the price system offers incentives to privilege actions which will ensure that further actions and options for action are aligned with the price system. That is why the patterns generated by this practice do not reflect an organization that is goal-directed, purposeful, and governed by a hierarchy of aims. They have the character, rather, of a spontaneous order or "catallaxy" which has a general purposefulness rather than pursuing any ultimate goal.[5] Market competition comes close to providing something that is actually impossible: a providential overview. And what presides over everything here, time and again, is Adam Smith's invisible hand: it is the system of prices and payments that produces expectable expectations and brings about a reciprocal adjustment of individual plans; it is the price system that coordinates demand and supply and sets up "self-organizing systems" by means of negative feedback; and it is the price system, finally, that directs the impersonal, noncoercive force of competition and brings about, if not a stable equilibrium, then at least an unsteady approximation to such an optimal state.

Two different aspects of this idea of competition are worth noting. On the one hand, the rationality of economic transactions is reinscribed here in a new code: the exchange "mechanism" becomes the "web" of competition. Competitive societies are understood as being defined less by reciprocal trade relations—as was still the case in the eighteenth century—than by competitive differences or inequalities. And whereas the market once fulfilled the (liberal) natural law of self-interest, it now follows the (neoliberal) idea or form (*ēidos*) of competition. Competition is declared the "soul" of the economy, the "life-spirit" of production, an all-determining principle of "gravitation" in the market, as it were.[6] And it characteristically enjoys a formal privilege insofar as it coincides with an order that can persist through change, even if it may only approximately, to a greater or lesser extent, maintain itself in a state of equilibrium. Competition is thus the kind of abstract ideal that is only more or less evident in actual market events. And this means, on the other hand, that competition is not a fundamental state of affairs but must be established, promoted, facilitated, and accomplished.[7] Competition does not exist already; it is a historical goal which requires proactive and resolute policy-making. It calls for a government that dictates the rules of the game, ensures they are observed, and encourages players to participate. Its freedom is not conditional on the weakness or absence of state controls; on the contrary, to gain real historical ground it depends on political vigilance and state intervention. Competitive societies must continually manage and enforce the conditions for competition and rivalry. And what has for some time been called "deregulation" always goes back to an ensemble of forceful interventions.

Physicalism

The second consequence is that the liberal oikodicy—with its invisible hands and balancing forces—is bound up with the use of a discourse that can only be called "physicalist." This term not only expresses the hope that political economy could become a positive science, a value-neutral scientific institution on the model of physics.[8] It also suggests how the history of political economy is punctuated at key moments by ideas of economic functioning that are directly modeled on natural laws. The drives of divergent interests were thought to be coordinated by the same laws as Newtonian gravity, for example, while the circulation of goods and money was understood, from the eighteenth century right up to the twentieth, in terms of the hydrodynamics of currents, characterized as a system of communicating vessels, pipes, wells, and tanks. There are also clear links between energetics and the neoclassical school, while the marginalist renewal of political economy oriented itself toward the treatment of variation and limit problems in the natural sciences. A final example is furnished by statistical mechanics and stochastics, which acquired renewed relevance in the latter half of the twentieth century thanks to discussion of random movement and probability on financial markets.[9]

In all such cases we are not merely dealing with analogies and metaphoric transfers, nor does political economy simply borrow images from the natural sciences. Correspondences of this kind reveal an essential motive for the increasing mathematization of economic science since the nineteenth century. In searching for a way to formulate rules for maintaining equilibrium, political economy was inspired by the natural sciences and responded by having recourse to mathematical models. By investigating the problem of how different volumes, quantities, and interactions can be represented in their interdependence and balance, and by pursuing the question of how equilibrium and stability in complex economic exchange relations are at all possible, the discourse of political economy crossed the threshold to formalization and moved asymptotically closer to mathematical physics.

If since the nineteenth century economic knowledge has thus shown a tendency not only to adopt the trappings of a science but also to formalize its axioms, this is essentially due to its assumption that there is a rational force for order at work in market events and to its trust in the market's capacity for homeostasis. The "beauty" of the system is on the line here. Political economy was established as a general theory of equilibrium and adduces the ability of the market to solve problems of disequilibrium as evidence for the truth of this theory. For a theory of economic dynamics, this means that its concepts and criteria must have the capacity to describe adequately a given state of the system at any particular point in time and therefore reliably predict future system-states. This requirement or theoretical profile probably also accounts for the astonishing durability of Newtonian semantics in economic theory. Newtonian mechanics was considered exemplary for such a long time because, in yielding knowledge about the current state and momentum of bodies, it could be used to depict all future conditions, dynamics, and system-states as well. It is therefore hardly surprising that orthodox economics continued to cling to analogies drawn from the equilibrium theories of physics even when physics itself had already taken leave of the principles of classical dynamics and, since the end of the nineteenth century, had begun to doubt the homogeneity of integrable physical systems.[10]

The idea that balancing forces are inherent to market activity is therefore more than a helpful simplification or, perhaps, a utopian substrate. Even if it is not really possible to know whether real economies actually tend toward balance, assumptions about equilibrium must be seen as a logical or theoretical necessity. The systematic nature of economic science could not have been guaranteed without such assumptions, nor could a coherent field of objects requiring economic analysis have been constituted. In fact, modern political economy would have no claim to epistemological coherence without the formally elaborated proof that "perfect competition" prevails in an "ideally decentralized economy" and that the behavior of economic players can be deduced from "axioms of rationality."[11] A "theory" of pure imbalance would make as little sense as the idea of a system without coherence or an axiomatic conception of irrationality. The various physicalisms, together with the transformation of economic science into a branch of applied mathematics, thus affirm the reality of self-balancing markets and permit the lasting self-assertion of economic theory *as* theory. This is how the system projects its essential claim to truth. And here, too, the oikodicy prevails, that is, the idea of the purposeful arrangement of the economic (capitalist) universe.

Credit economy

To be sure, this has never excluded the possibility that the idol of an efficient market society, the equilibrium theorem in all its variants, could be assailed by constant doubts, nor that it could be described as a "fruitful error," pure "illusion," a "scientific riddle," ludicrously inadequate, or even as "the most remarkable error in the history of economic theory," little more than a "de-cerebration machine."[12] It might be asked whether the chance attribution of quantification and measurability to specific social phenomena justifies a strict dichotomy of economic and non-economic facts; we might inquire, too, whether political economy is willing and able to exercise adequate oversight in relation to how it selects its key assumptions and data. But even if we set aside these questions, doubts have been entertained for some time now as to whether the evolutionary fable of the market, with its narrative arc leading from exchange or competition to equilibrium, is really capable of encompassing elemental, endogenous processes of contemporary and modern economic activity. It seems doubtful, then, whether a theoretical science of economic dynamics is at all possible within a classical or neoclassical conceptual framework. There is a disturbance or rift in this discourse relating to an essential element of capitalist economies: the logic of capital and credit systems.

The development of trade and commerce was undoubtedly directly bound up with the emergence of a credit economy, with the use of promissory notes, deposit receipts, and bonds, with banking practices and the possibility of transferring undertakings to pay rather than having always to pay upfront. Since the Middle Ages, the rudiments of a functioning credit system have been necessary conditions for the expansion of commercial capitalism.[13] It is all the more surprising, then, that it was not until the end of the eighteenth century that a sufficiently systematic discussion of banking, capital, and credit mechanisms got underway. This may be due to a delay in the emergence of a systematic science of economics, which was notoriously late in catching up with manifest business practices; but it may also have owed something to a certain theoretical resistance to the fact that a genuinely capitalist structure—one that trades with credit, assets, prospective profits, and hence with time—could no longer be directly translated back into elementary exchange and balance relations. Though people still assumed that there was a balancing dynamic at work in the market, the constant circulation of debt, credit, and capital they observed seemed to contradict this assumption, and they were evidently alarmed by the wide-ranging impact of the economic decisions and actions being taken.

A financial event that took place toward the end of the eighteenth century may be regarded as a kind of primal scene for this disquiet. The event in question involved one of the most important financial institutions and led to an all but unprecedented innovation in finance policy. We are dealing with an exemplary situation: toward the end of the eighteenth century the Bank of England became the subject of a discussion from which a number of questions emerged about the extent to which concepts of balance and equilibrium are fit to capture the dynamics of modern capital transactions.

The Bank of England

The Bank was founded in 1694 in response to deep-seated anxiety about the economy and has been a source of lasting irritation ever since. An early example of such irritation is provided by the strange figure introduced to readers of *The Spectator* by Joseph Addison in 1711: a virgin who allegorically refers to the predicament in which the new institution found itself at the time. "Seated on a Throne of Gold," she is presented—in keeping with contemporary convention—as a hypochondriac who is "troubled with Vapors." Her constitution is so delicate that the various objects and incidents she encounters in the scene bring about "quick Turns and Changes" in her condition, from "a wasting Distemper" to "the highest Health and Vigor," from faintness to attentiveness, from a ruddy to a pallid complexion. She first casts her eye over texts hung on the walls and "written in Golden Letters": the Magna Carta, the Act of Uniformity, the Act of Toleration—all Acts of Parliament that can be scrutinized with "Pleasure" or "Uneasiness." She pays particular attention to "a Couple of Secretaries" seated at her feet, who read to her news "from all Parts of the World." As she listens to their reports, the allegorical figure displays "Symptoms of Health or Sickness" in swift succession, wasting away from "the most healthful state of Body" into a "Skeleton" before making no less sudden a recovery. She is especially terrified by the "Phantoms" of anarchy, tyranny, bigotry, and atheism that parade before her. This finally leads to a fatal darkening of the scene itself: the sacks of gold surrounding the throne are suddenly transformed into "Bags full of Wind," while gold coins turn into mere paper. Addison leaves us in no doubt about what the virgin represents: she bears the title "Publick Credit" and is seated in a chamber that unmistakably resembles the business premises of the Bank of England in London.[14]

Even if Addison's personification of public credit always recovers from her tribulations, her situation and her mission remain precarious: only with great difficulty can she preserve her virtue and her threatened innocence in the midst of all the commercial activities and misfortunes swirling around her. As well as alluding to contemporary party-political conflicts, Addison's text brings together a number of questions that deeply implicate the procedures of the Bank of England—indeed the nature of banking itself—and have preoccupied political economy since the end of the seventeenth century. In the first place we are asked to consider the principles on which the Bank itself was founded. Following the example of the Amsterdam Exchange Bank and conscious of initiating a new project, the Bank of England was selected from a wide array of possible business models. Some seventy different revenue-raising ventures were mooted at the time, ranging from lotteries to corporations, from tax increases to banking institutes. The Bank was set up to service the debts contracted by the royal family and to cover their capital needs. One of the initiators of the project, the merchant William Paterson, began circulating various petitions about the project from the beginning of the 1690s. Although motivated by a number of interests, he had one particular aim in mind: to legalize the predatory actions of a rapacious monarchy. By 1640, Charles I had already commandeered approximately 200,000 pounds sterling in coins and precious metal belonging to the merchants of London. In 1672 Charles II repudiated the Crown's accumulated debts and thus placed the financial reputation of the kingdom in jeopardy. The English monarch had repeatedly confiscated valuables belonging to citizens and merchants which had been deposited in the Tower or treasury. At Paterson's suggestion, this perennial princely theft was transformed into a contract between debtor and creditors: the king was simply given an advance of £1.2 million and charged 8 percent interest on the loan. Along with the various other experiments in procuring money, the Bank of England was established as a clear consequence of state bankruptcy and an act of fiscal despair. It was essential to establish a reliable and contractually binding relationship with the Crown, so this became one of the main clauses in the charter of the new bank.[15] At the same time, the bank was intended to facilitate the management of financial matters on the emerging world market and provide the capital needed for overseas trade and colonial affairs; from the very beginning this bank, like the Exchange Bank of Amsterdam before it, was designed as a vital switch point in a wide-ranging network of global subsidiaries and information routes.

The economy of the seventeenth century showed the first signs of movement toward globalization, and the risks likewise assumed global dimensions. As the author of *Ephemera of Humankind* wrote in 1776, the mistakes of a Chinese government minister could plunge all Europe into chaos.[16] Such interdependencies brought with them a particular danger that, more than any other, was causing Addison's allegorical figure to "faint and dye away," a danger that explains the sense of agitation animating his text and that effects the sudden transformation of money into air and gold into paper at the end. What Addison addresses here as the "Specter" of banking, capital markets, and commercial activity derives from a basic principle of Enlightenment financial and semiotic policy: the principle that circulating signs—promissory notes, bank notes, loans on credit, IOUs, and so on—must remain covered by their equivalent in precious metals and valuables, that these signs represent value and are held in balance only to the extent that they are tied to and controlled by a treasury of signifieds. Only with reference to such a hoard of secure assets—typically, gold or silver—can circulating monetary symbols be kept in a state of equilibrium.

In characterizing the economic-cum-political program of the Enlightenment, the problem of credit, and the work of the Bank of England, Addison's condensed and suggestive allegory thus identifies the following four functions or principles: a contractually binding, mutual arrangement that included even the king himself and established a kind of *contrat social*; a steering mechanism that navigated reliably through immensely complex networks and unknown relationships of dependence; a politics of symbols that found nothing more abominable than empty, windy signifiers devoid of all reference to reality; and finally, a circulation of monetary signs that were firmly anchored in real fixed assets, thereby guaranteeing parity and balance in commercial exchange. By satisfying all four principles, the Bank of England and the institution of the National Debt were to occupy a strategically and symbolically central position at the center of London, providing a mainstay for the kingdom's continued political and economic power.

Quite unexpectedly, a private institution had succeeded in acquiring a political role. In keeping with a parallel shift in the institution of the monarchy itself, the spirit of the "common wealth" now had its seat in the

Bank of England. As Daniel Defoe wrote in 1710, public credit "is not the effect of this or that wheel in the government moving regular and just to its proper work but of the whole movement"; it results from the interplay between the monarch and the parliament, between "exact, punctual management" and good business.[17] The Bank of England and public credit thus stand for the political and economic interconnections of everything with everything else, and it is perfectly consistent with this interpretation to see the allegorical body of the virgin as another of the king's bodies.

1797

A century later, both this new order and the innocence of the allegorical lady were in grave danger. Both were finally and irrevocably lost, and this loss suggests the despoliation of a political and economic idyll. Two etchings made by James Gillray in 1797 point to this conclusion. One depicts public credit as a woman of now advanced years sitting on a treasure chest; she appears scandalized by the unwelcome attentions of a young gallant, the thirty-seven-year-old William Pitt, who had been British prime minister since 1783. The victim's cries for help—"Murder! Murder! Theft! Murder! O you blackguard! Have I guarded my treasure for so long, only to have it finally stolen by you? Murder! Theft! Shame! Ruin! Ruin! Ruin!"—lead us directly to the subject of the second caricature. It depicts a figure representing public credit towering over the dome of the Bank of England, a Midas with a churning stomach who turns everything he touches not into gold but, fatally, into paper. It would appear that in 1797 the Bank of England had lost its virtue, its chastity, and its politico-economic dignity—and this misfortune can only be understood as a caesura in the functioning of political economy and as an *epoché* for economic science as such. What then lay behind the commotion reflected in Gillray's caricatures? What unprecedented state of affairs do they thematize? What disturbance or controversy is expressed here in the discourse of political economy? And in what respect can we speak here of a primal scene of finance economics?

The answers to these questions are to be found in an event that occurred over two separate days in February 1797. On February 4, 1797, the French project for funding the revolution and financing the state by

FIGURE I   James Gillray, "Political Ravishment, or The Lady of Threadneedle Street in Danger!" May 22, 1797.

issuing *assignats*—certificates representing the value of confiscated church properties—had to be declared a failure. This paper money had undergone such rapid devaluation that it had sunk within a few years of its first being issued in 1789 to just 0.5 percent of its nominal value. In the end, it could only represent the incapacity of the revolutionary government to cover its expenses. It seems all the more astonishing that at almost exactly the same time another financial event was unfolding across the English Channel which stood at once in strict analogy and in stark contrast to this collapse. Repeatedly described by contemporaries as "incredible," "disturbing," and "extremely concerning," perceived as an unprecedented and deeply alarming event, as "the most frightening thing that can possibly be imagined," and yet at the same time as "one of the finest things this century has witnessed in the field of national economics," the incident in question was evidently taken to usher in a new era in the use of economic signs.[18] It took place in the same noteworthy month of February 1797, this time on the twenty-sixth, when the Bank of England was absolved

MIDAS, *Transmuting all into* ~~GOLD~~ PAPER.

FIGURE 2   James Gillray, "Midas, Transmuting All into ~~Gold~~ Paper," 1797.

by parliamentary decree of the obligation to change bank notes back into coins. Henceforth, it no longer had to guarantee ongoing cover for the paper money in circulation.

What came to pass was the exact opposite of the tragic and ruinous ending to the French experiment with *assignats*. For the unprecedented aspect of this economic and legal operation was that the refusal to pay in metal coinage amounted to a refusal to pay at all. In effect, a new financial system was set up precisely on the basis of insolvency and in the absence of any reference to real wealth. This posed a new challenge for economic analysis and perhaps also revealed a rift in the foundations of economic science itself. The challenge was to think through what it meant that although one cannot, say, ride a claim to a horse, one *can* make payments on the strength of a mere claim to money.[19] Nothing less was at the forefront of one commentator's mind when he heralded the decision by the Bank of England as a "great" and as yet "insufficiently valued world event," an instantiation of the fiscal sublime.[20] And this is the remarkable point of fact: whereas the insolvency of the French state spelled an end to the *assignats* project, England's inability to pay—resulting from the drain on treasury funds caused by the Coalition Wars—had exactly the opposite effect: it was the precondition and starting point for the intervention pushed by Pitt which led, not to a collapse in prices but to a mild economic recovery. French observers were astonished that "the most important quarrel that a nation can possibly have with the shareholders, administrators and creditors of a bank was amicably concluded in two days, as though it were a transaction carried out within a family."[21]

Assignats

Clearly, two similar, comparable, and yet utterly divergent paper money systems came together here at one and the same point in time. Each reflected a different economic infrastructure; each functioned in different ways; and—most importantly—each embodied an utterly different understanding of monetary, financial, and symbolic transactions. The failed French experiment in financing state debt led many contemporaries to recall the paper money project devised by the infamous economist and schemer, John Law, to avert state bankruptcy following the death of Louis XIV. Law's scheme involved a complicated system of land mortgages, joint-stock companies, and paper currency—and in this he is said to have been one of the models for Mephistopheles in *Faust, Part II.* The way in which the French system was handled, both theoretically and practically, also directly recapitulates a number of the basic principles from eighteenth-century theories about the circulation of money. *First,* it was above all the question of how to cover borrowings that inspired thinking about the quality of paper money. On the one hand, the *assignats* were issued as bonds on confiscated church property and supposedly enjoyed the advantage—as John Law had already argued—of not being exposed, like mere cash, to fluctuations in the price of precious metals. Unencumbered by any intrinsic market value, they were free to stimulate circulation as additional means of exchange and as "tokens." On the other hand, if doubts were to arise as to whether they could be redeemed or converted into real assets, they would turn into pretend money or fictitious signs, pure and simple. As their representative power became uncertain or weakened or faded away altogether, they would stand revealed as a "meaningless" substitute, testifying to nothing but their own lack of reality and value: "Every kind of property can be represented by paper money.. . . . Whoever issues paper money must have the property it represents in his possession, so he does not find himself dispensing the sign without having the thing it signifies."[22] One of the first problems associated with the *assignats*, as indeed with eighteenth-century monetary transactions in general, thus lies in the representative power of signs: the question, that is, of how tenuous or secure, narrow or broad-based is the link to an asset that can guarantee its value, whether this be bullion, treasury funds, or—as in the case of the *assignats*—confiscated land.

    Second, for this symbolic system it is important that the sum of issued *assignats* matches the value of the assets they denote, so that no "artificial" wealth is created exceeding the "natural" wealth represented in this way. Only strict proportionality in the relation between the numerical value of the signs and the worth of the underlying assets can guarantee steady circulation and hence ensure that the balance between monetary symbols and real property is maintained. These symbols would be unable to circulate if their value were disproportionate to the assets they represent. And it is worth noting that two hopes were nurtured in vain by orthodox quantity theory right up to the end of the period of *assignats* economics: the hope that the notes in circulation would appreciate in value if fewer notes were issued, and the inverse hope that raising their price would bring about a proportionate increase in revenue.[23] The crux of the *assignats* system was thus identified in the question of how the notes could be transformed into substantial value, so preserving a balance between fictitious signs and real assets. This question goes to the heart of Enlightenment quantity theory: representative signs must be numerically proportionate to the wealth they represent if equilibrium is to be maintained.

Third and finally, a specific legal form is connected both with the nature of *assignats* as pledges and with the monetary theories of the Enlightenment. Just as, in the eighteenth century, money was nothing but a sign that could reliably be exchanged for a predetermined quantity of goods and assets, so the value of notes was determined by the pledge to return the equivalent of their printed value into their owner's hands. Intrinsic value, the promise of payment, and—as in the case of the *assignats*—legal decree could all equally vouch for and guarantee the security of the notes.

Thanks to the example of the *assignats*, this very promise was now treated as problematic from both an economic and a political point of view. Condorcet, for example, noted a fundamental ambiguity in the economic character of *assignats* as redeemable tokens. Either they can be understood as interest-bearing fixed-term loans, in which case they are tied to specific redemption dates, or they are nothing but paper money and means of payment requiring immediate redemption on demand: there is confusion about the nature and term of the future transaction being promised here. According to Condorcet (among others), the *assignats'* fatal flaw was that they contained two incompatible and contradictory promises. They therefore raised general doubts about whether the revolutionary government could be trusted to keep its word. At the same time, they could still be understood in terms of a key concept in social contract theory, the legal obligation to reciprocity, which allowed the new paper money to appear as "indestructible cement" for the new constitutional order. At best, this meant that the legal order and the contractual obligations written into the constitution were themselves circulated along with the *assignats* and distributed among the entire nation, so that "all citizens would have an

equal interest in preserving and defending them."[24] At worst, however—
and this counterargument was not long in coming—these same pieces of
paper were shown up to be "artificial cement" as soon as they depreciated,
causing the nation of *citoyens* to degenerate into a rabble of "speculators"
and "gamesters." According to Edmund Burke, the collapse of the *assignats* would bring the constitution and its system of law and order down
with them—and the achievements of the revolution itself would simply
drain away.[25]

This means, in short, that the representative power of paper money,
the equilibrium between signs and riches, and the legal guarantee of the
government's pledge formed the coordinates around which arguments and
counterarguments about the *assignats* were plotted. Even in 1797, the *assignats* were still being debated against the background of Enlightenment
theories of money and framed by conceptions of natural law and rational-
ism. Their collapse can thus only be understood as a devaluation of the
government's word, signifying a failure of will attesting to the political
undependability of the *volonté générale*.

Bank notes

Reflections on the decision made by the Bank of England in February 1797 took quite a different course. John Law's old project now
appeared in a new light, suggesting a promising precedent for the current
finance-political undertaking. It became apparent that the criteria mentioned above for passing judgment on the *assignats* were of little use in
explaining how English bank notes functioned. Since Addison, images of
puffing and swelling had dominated the metaphorical language used to
describe paper money, imagery which recurred in the windbags of "inflation" (from the Latin *flare*, to blow). Yet the same windy emptiness that
had once signaled the deficiency of both Law's paper securities and the
assignats—their combination of legal tender and bonds in a single certificate—now defined the status of the notes issued by the London bank.
Once the requirement to exchange circulating bank notes for metal currency was dropped, the notes became both at once: as legal tender, they
were mere substitutes for circulating coinage; as bonds, they served only
to document that there was presently nothing to hand for which they

could be exchanged. On the one hand, then, they guaranteed the right to redeem deposited assets and sums of money; on the other, they functioned as currency only if that entitlement was waived. While bank notes originally had the legal standing of a deposit certificate and contract serving—as in the English goldsmith's note—as a receipt for deposited valuables, monetary transactions could only be sustained by forgoing this contractual arrangement. In the words of one of the first theorists of credit, "All the cash in the world would not satisfy claims of this sort, if all men having a right to urge them, were disposed to do so."[26]

A bank note—this fact came to light in February 1797, at the latest—is not simply symbolic money or a paper substitute for currency. It can no longer be understood as a promise redeemable under natural and contractual law, or at best only in a paradoxical way. It stands both for the promise of a certain sum of money and for the failure of that promised sum to materialize. This paradoxical structure is its distinguishing feature; it is a hybrid for which there was as yet no concise term in 1800. It has an economic side (in the form of credit) and a legal side (in the form of cash payment). As a credit instrument it requires the deferral of payment, yet as legal tender it calls for immediate redemption; as a substitute for money it needs to be fully backed, yet as a bill of credit it rules out that very possibility. It is at once money and the promise of money, and its semiotic structure is marked by the way it encompasses a "here" (*da*) and a "gone" (*fort*) in one and the same act: a self-referential paradox that tightens as it pulls solvency and insolvency together. Strictly speaking, it is therefore not a second kind of money; rather, it is the "*most effective*" credit instrument because, as "the *most susceptible of being circulated*," it does away with the need for money altogether. It contains the contradiction that "results from the unification of the characteristics and functions of a credit instrument and currency in one and the same note."[27]

Accordingly, around 1800 we see considerable terminological efforts being made to clarify that, unlike in the case of the *assignats*, it is precisely the fictitious or "chimerical"—that is, unbacked—character of bank notes that makes payment possible, so attesting to their ambiguous position. This gave rise to much casuistry:

If ... the token being used has no intrinsic value, or is not accompanied by the customary security and serviceability, it unmistakably lacks an essential requirement of legitimate payment. However, we must proceed carefully when applying this essentially correct principle. For there will always be a prospect that the paper tokens can be cashed in for their real value; here the state will extend such a prospect by issuing instructions for future redemption, there it will be given by the subscribing public. And since this latter prospect can be considered certain—at least as far as payment into public coffers is concerned—we cannot really claim that intrinsic value is completely lacking, in the strict sense of the word, when we pay with paper tokens; that would definitely be an injustice. Nevertheless, this assured prospect can be so severely limited, and the uncertain one so distant and wide, that they can at times be considered negligible. In these circumstances it is possible to assert—though not in the form of a definitive judgment, which is never permissible in the absence of fully defined concepts— that payments made with paper tokens under conditions of great uncertainty concerning the prospect of their intrinsic value being realized, whether through redemption or through payment in kind, may well be in accordance with existing civil law but are in violation of natural rights.[28]

Convoluted discussions of this kind show how commentators were beginning to think through the mechanisms of public credit and capital transactions. In doing so, they focused their attention less on acts of exchange and the balancing powers of the market than on the irritating factors of uncertainty, potential outlooks, and future expectations.

Temporalization

Backed or unbacked, possessing intrinsic value or lacking it, fit or unfit to serve as a means of payment, honored at face value or debased, legal tender or unlawful currency: the difficulty of grappling conceptually with public credit derives from the contradictory functions that came into effect with the Bank of England's decision. The perplexity and tortuousness evident in contemporary formulations arose from the mix of credit notes and money in circulation. In view of this hybrid, it is no accident that later commentators could speak of the first theories of credit, proclaiming a "new era" of monetary theories that attempted to resolve such paradoxes and thus stood for a reformed science of commercial transactions. These paradoxes were resolved by a thoroughgoing "temporalization" of the system.[29] The circulation of something that is by its very nature absent can only be explained as the effect of an endless deferral, ruling out full, universal compensation for the debts in question. Chains of payment had now become chains of payment promises; every operation seems to anticipate an open future and break up a formerly closed circle of reciprocity. Solvency and insolvency, the capacity and incapacity to pay circulate to the same extent and guarantee the continued functioning of the system by ensuring that every transaction raises the prospect of an indefinite number of further transactions.

The measures introduced by the Bank of England in February 1797 to create value through credit, thereby conveniently allowing this watershed in financial politics and discourse history to be fixed to a point in time, effectively discredited the equilibrium ideas, zero-sum game, and quantity theorem of the older monetary doctrines. Thanks to deferred backing, unequal proportions, and a lack of equilibrium, creditors and debtors now have the same amount of money at their disposal de jure. Now everyone can own something only "to the extent that he is owned in turn," and it is agreed that every payment is an (unredeemable) promise to pay, that everything we have does not really belong to us, that all excess is really scarcity, every oversupply a shortfall, and that the complete collapse of the system can only be avoided by its endless continuation. In other words, deferral must always be possible[30]—a constitutive disequilibrium in the system driving it towards an open future. Time has become a productive factor, and in view of the temporal structure of credit, attempts to back it with goods or metal coinage appear at the very least to be illogical.

In retrospect, it was precisely the conditions under which the French *assignats* system was established and which it reflected that doomed it to failure. Three explanations can now be offered for the dramatic depreciation of the state-sponsored paper money: first, it depended on confiscated goods for security; second, it was conceived as standing in a proportionate relationship to metal currency; third, it was unallied to a policy of public credit.[31] The representative character of signs now stands opposed to their temporalized self-referentiality. Two apparently analogous yet irreconcilable perspectives are juxtaposed here. In the eighteenth century, economic science could not really differentiate between paper money and bank notes, attributing the representative power of the sign to both, so all the developments that by February 1797 had determined how modern paper currency was to function—temporalization, deferred backing, and circulating credit—were inevitably experienced as a crisis. The self-referential nature of the system made itself felt as a ruinous loss of referentiality.

This divergence, together with the *epoché* of economic science around 1800 that it helped exacerbate, could not have been manifested any more clearly: just as Napoleon purported to read the future collapse of England in the English bank notes (and maintained bullion reserves for his military campaigns), so Prime Minister Pitt foresaw the future collapse of France in the *assignats*.[32] This confrontation of French *assignats* and English bank notes dramatizes a transformation in economic semiosis and probably even in semiotic codification itself. Whereas it was still possible, in the period from John Law's schemes to the *assignats* debacle, to detect a risky transformation of assets into chimeras and shadows, a substitution of mere smoke and mirrors for the things themselves,[33] the same metamorphoses had by 1800 become functionalized. The representative power of the sign has been relocated: it now lies in the capacity to facilitate transfers through self-reference. Money is credit and hence the promise of money; it dissolves the symmetry of exchange and counterexchange. If terms such as "pledge" and "reciprocity" are still applicable here, then the pledge appears to be as binding as it is untenable. At no point can it seem possible for the pledge to be redeemed, so that once given, it could "circulate for a hundred years without even once being realized as metal currency."[34] If credit money enacts a promise, it is a promise that revokes itself in the giving.

Credo of capital

Toward the end of the eighteenth century, the manner in which public credit and capital functioned had thus become problematic, challenging a number of the basic assumptions of political economy. These early attempts at formulating a theory of credit describe procedures for bringing money into circulation without it ever having to change hands. They circle around the mystery of a kind of transubstantiation associated with liquidity procurement and—as far as credit is concerned—with a creation ex nihilo. They note an ever-increasing variety of payment instruments and a money supply that has freed itself from the supply of circulating commodities. In all this, we can see the beginnings of a revolution in finance that invests unproductive money with procreative power and drives the circulation of capital through the selling of debt.

This means, firstly, that the sphere of circulation becomes autonomous, detaches itself from the sphere of production, and is now subject only to its own laws; it can no longer be converted into simple acts of exchange. Payments are open promises to pay; and unlike the circulation of mere money, that of credit and capital is independent of existing commodities or the limits of available money.[35] A new syntactic structure or chain, M-C-M (Money–Commodity–Money), replaces the C-M-C transaction; expressed in more recent terminology, not only is the self-referential nature of finance institutionalized, but we can also detect an autopoietic closure of the system, such that every payment is now made on condition that the string of payments can be extended indefinitely into the future. The credit economy becomes a prerequisite for the circulation of money and shapes its capitalist structure. To the extent that a new dimension becomes apparent in capital transactions and in emerging finance markets, the earlier concern with "correct" valuations and assured references to assets becomes obsolete. The distinction between real and fictitious values, natural and artificial wealth, material and immaterial goods, the real and the virtual economy makes little sense here. One could almost speak of a Romantic commercial profile: premised on the paradox of "self-guaranteeing money," the circulation of credit proves to be the setting for a kind of "poetry" (or "enabling fiction") that allows the circulation of mere illusions to determine economic relations.[36]

There emerges—secondly—a boundless, excessive, and self-perpetuating movement. This economy interrupts the closed circle of debt and repayment by resorting to an indefinite deferral that introduces time as a decentering factor. Circulation does not involve a series of progressive compensations but rather the endless proliferation of a nondischargeable debt. As a result of this temporalization, which makes available what is unavailable, interminability is programmed into the functional operations of the system. Time is out of joint. Capital transactions are determined by their fixation on the future; the future itself becomes a productive force and from now on makes the finance and credit economy the benchmark of economic modernization as such.

In all these aspects we can detect an upheaval in discourse that characterizes economic science around 1800. The status of public credit, the creation of money out of nothing, the continuous transmission of debt, and thus the logic of capital can no longer be traced back—in a genetic or evolutionary sense—to any exchange mechanism. The dynamics of the credit economy are incommensurable with the mechanisms of the material and monetary economy; they do not operate with existing quantities or sums. The element of time in credit has not only become a new criterion for economic science; it has raised doubts about the very scientificity of that science. These doubts eat away at the atemporal relations of exchange and counterexchange, balance and reciprocity, and closed circularity. With the time of capital, reflection on the economy as a system shifts to expectations, limited time frames, and uncertain futures, and thus to a kind of agitation which manifests itself as a weakening in the stability of self-balancing systems.[37] What keeps this system moving is its very *lack* of equilibrium.

From now on, in any case, the doctrines of political economy are assailed by questions about whether and in what way monetary surrogates take on monetary functions; whether they have to be stabilized by convertibility, substantial assets, and precious metal standards; whether and in what way market forces correspond to the forces of financial markets; and finally, whether and in what way the mechanisms of the capital and credit economy "automatically" tend toward balance. Credit is not just one type of monetary transaction among others but the insubstantial essence of all such transactions. As the "credo of capital" (Marx), public credit calls into question the chief tenet of the liberal oikodicy and encourages reasonable doubt about the balancing powers of the market. Subjected to questions of finance economics, the equilibrium models for which political economy is notorious lose their reliable, quasi-natural authority.

Idyll of the Market II

The epoch of the finance economy

It becomes possible to speak of primal scenes of capital and financial revolutions at the point where debt cycles begin to drive the creation of money. This was already happening in a systematic way in commercial practice in the seventeenth-century Netherlands; and we can see, if we take the Bank of England as an example, that it led toward the end of the eighteenth century not only to the first theories of credit but also to perceptions of an epochal change in economic transactions. Here a categorical distinction between the monetary economy and the credit economy first became apparent, each with its own distinct mechanisms, parameters, and semiotic operations. In the process, time became an essential determining factor in economics; temporality is stretched out from a circle or cycle to a line extending indefinitely into the future. Divergent ideas about the representation of wealth generated a certain ambivalence in the science of political economy, which found expression in two different schools of thought. Whereas one saw gold and silver bullion and bank reserves as providing an essential guarantee for the quasi-automatic balancing of the currency system, the other took the exact opposite view, insisting that the stability of money and monetary surrogates resides independently in the functioning of the business cycle.[1] In any case, within a few decades the Bank of England had resumed cash payments and reaffirmed the convertibility of bank notes, with the result that the metal or gold standard acquired an almost mythological significance for ideas of monetary equilibrium in the nineteenth and twentieth centuries.[2]

Given all this, it is hardly surprising that such periodic controversies and the questions they raised decided how the epoch-making character of economic systems and financial measures would be viewed from then on. We can see a new and particularly striking example of this in the 1960s and 1970s, when a constellation emerged that can be interpreted as a reprisal and variation of the "Romantic" situation that obtained around 1800. Here, too, observers registered a "financial revolution" or "historical watershed," a "significant discontinuity in the history of money," an "unprecedented situation," a "unique" event and turning point—in short, they heralded the dawning of a new era in the history of finance.[3] They also, once again, gave voice to concerns and expectations relating to the mechanisms of money circulation, value guarantees, and the dynamics of balancing processes. If we care to draw an analogy with the discourse situation in the Romantic era, then it lies in how both came to terms with a crisis of representation.

The story of the debates about the end of the Bretton Woods Agreement is a familiar one and has been told many times before. Against the backdrop of the Great Depression, the various interwar crises, and the war economy, representatives of forty-four nations met at Mount Washington Hotel in Bretton Woods, New Hampshire, on July 23, 1944, to discuss a raft of measures for restructuring the economy after the war. The Agreement produced institutions such as the International Monetary Fund, the World Bank, and the General Agreement on Tariffs and Trade (which later became the World Trade Organization), all of which arose in response to the demand for an active financial policy. With a view to stabilizing international payments, ensuring the unlimited convertibility of currencies, and promoting the unimpeded circulation of goods and capital, the production of reliable exchange rates was tied to a fixed financial mechanism; hence, a gold standard was established at the same time. All participating countries were required to peg their currencies at fixed exchange rates to the world's strongest currency, the US dollar, which in turn was tied to gold at a fixed rate. What was now nominally a gold-backed system (although in reality a gold-dollar system) was in turn bound up with the postulate of an elementary equilibrium that rested, in the end, on the self-correcting effect of the exchangeability of money and gold. With the dollar mediating, the gold standard thus assumed a kind of anchoring function, neutralizing any potential disturbances in the system by means of a mechanism for adjusting money supply to prices.[4]

In the voluminous literature on Bretton Woods, the Agreement has been judged in many different ways: as a productive innovation, a historical necessity, a provisional arrangement, an economic enigma, or simply as a project that was politically and economically stillborn. However, there is general consensus that it represented a difficult, incoherent, or even impossible compromise between incompatible positions. It sought to reconcile the gold guarantee with currency parity, balancing mechanisms, foreign currency restrictions, and flexible exchange rates. A number of circumstances arose after the establishment of the Bretton Woods system to undermine its effectiveness, provoke various doubts about its regulatory ideas, and make its demise foreseeable. These included the increasing mobility of international capital and an expansive US monetary policy; accumulating foreign dollar assets and a mounting US deficit because of the Vietnam war; the quest for higher capital returns on investments due to declining profit margins in American industries; the mismatch between American liabilities and gold reserves; and the difficulty in sustaining a fixed gold price. A further weakness was identified in the unwieldy organizational apparatus that made it necessary for agreements to be struck continuously between governments and central banks.

It is no accident that an all but typical financial controversy became apparent here: whereas those on one side of the debate decried their opponents' unfounded faith in dubious equilibrium theorems, those on the other side saw the effectiveness of balancing mechanisms being fatally undermined by institutional interference. The chronicle of the Bretton Woods stability agreement is therefore inevitably told as the story of its demise. As early as 1961, the industrialized nations had committed themselves to refrain from converting their US dollars into gold. Then, after the United States threatened to suspend the convertibility of the dollar altogether, a number of other member states were forced to appreciate their currencies, notably the Japanese yen and the Deutsche Mark. A significant outflow of dollars into Deutsche Marks followed in the spring of 1971, prompting both France and Great Britain to demand that dollar reserves be exchanged for gold. All these developments finally led President Nixon to order the symbolic closure of the so-called gold window on August 15, 1971.[5] Dollars ceased to be convertible, the gold standard became obsolete, and a little later, in 1973, the end of the Bretton Woods Agreement was formally sealed.

In retrospect, then, the adjustment mechanisms built into the Bretton Woods system seemed to indicate a flawed approach to financial markets; the gold standard itself appeared to be a mere illusion; and the economic policies propping it up looked like a last futile effort to secure the world monetary order by backing currencies with gold. A slow but irreversible transition was perceived in all this: from commodity-backed money to credit money, from a fully backed currency system to an unbacked one. By the end of Bretton Woods, unbacked paper money, or money on account, was no longer seen as a merely temporary expedient in times of crisis but as the precondition, functional element, and unavoidable destiny of international capital transactions. This is what justified the rhetoric of epochal change.

With the revocation of the Bretton Woods currency agreement, all formal ties to the US dollar and its gold anchor were annulled, leading analysts to claim that not only were post-war financial structures collapsing, but a previously inconceivable break in the 2,500-year history of money was also taking place. The radical step to cancel the direct convertibility of currency into gold seemed to signal nothing less than a "postmodern" caesura. It looked as if an economic *condition postmoderne* had arrived and was veering unsteadily toward a system of flexible and "floating" exchange rates, a regime of free-floating signifiers—anchorless and immeasurable—that lacked backing from any transcendental signified. This signaled "the rise of a system" that was held to be truly "unprecedented": a system in which currencies referred only to other currencies and were based, directly or indirectly, on a standard of unbacked fiat money.[6] The sporadic and local circulation of unredeemable payment promises that had characterized the credit scene around 1800 had now, a hundred and seventy years later, mutated into a global financial system that proved exemplary in dispensing altogether with any reference to value. This undoubtedly presented a new challenge to economic theory.

New liberalism

So long as dispute raged over whether the Bretton Woods Agreement had failed due to incoherent ideas of equilibrium or, on the contrary, due to excessive political interference with balancing processes, and so long as people puzzled over whether fixing currencies to the gold standard was an effective way of stabilizing the system, a useful fiction, a financial fetish, or simply a mistake, the 1970s could look like a period in which economic theory once again began to make history. That is apparent from the way in which, step by step, all the institutional and technical requirements were put in place for establishing an international financial system that still remains in force well into the twenty-first century. It holds particularly true for a laboratory-type situation in which economic processes stand revealed as applied economic theory, capital transactions as implemented monetary theory, and manifest market events as realizations of specific idols of the marketplace. The result was a field of experimentation—as theoretical as it was practical—in which new markets and market conditions were produced that were designed to demonstrate, once and for all, the internal consistency of the capitalist oikodicy.

The hour had struck for the system programs of neoliberalism. The end of Bretton Woods offered more than just the prospect of fluctuating exchange rates and monetary instability; it simultaneously held out the possibility of proving that a rational principle of order was at work precisely in the free play of market mechanisms. As early as the 1950s, Milton Friedman, preoccupied at the time with implementing the Marshall Plan in Europe, had written a note calling for the guidelines of the Bretton Woods Agreement to be abandoned and its commitment to fixed exchange rates dropped as a precondition for establishing genuine currency markets. After years spent endlessly restating the same idea, he reformulated this demand under changed circumstances in the autumn of 1971, in what was probably one of the simplest, shortest, and most influential papers in the history of economics.

Commissioned to write the paper by the Chicago Mercantile Exchange, Friedman presented an argument about the logic of future market developments with which other authorities in the field were in complete agreement. It can be summarized in the following terms. After

the end of the Bretton Woods Agreement, continuous exchange rate fluctuations and the resulting currency risks in international trade and capital
transactions have led to a precarious state of affairs. They generate not
only uncertainty and volatility but also high insurance costs for the parties
concerned. It is therefore appropriate to make available financial instruments that will delegate risk-minimization procedures entirely to market mechanisms themselves. This can only happen through the creation
of new finance markets and futures trading with shares and currencies.
Fluctuating exchange rates are to be secured or "hedged" with forward
exchange contracts; investors can insure themselves against possible price
differences by betting on such price differences. And if a speculative market based on the difference between current and future prices is created by
these means, the systematic realization and expansion of that market can
only have a balancing effect. Here the need for security goes hand in hand
with the search for opportunities to take risks and make profits; and "the
greater the volume of speculative activity," the more efficiently—"the better"—the market will function. A triple economic dilemma is thus resolved
at a stroke: it is precisely through liberal trade arrangements that exchange
rates and price levels are to be controlled. The market itself becomes liable
for the costs associated with currency risks; monetary policy is entrusted
to the movements of the market. The United States, in particular, appears
predestined to make this new order possible, for it is in this country that
the highest degree of liquidity in capital transactions is combined with a
long and glorious tradition of "free, open and fair markets."[7]

Friedman's little capitalist manifesto clearly defined expectations for
establishing new financial markets: hope for a system of stable exchange
rates is replaced by hope for a stable system of exchange rates. Once money
is based on trade with derivatives, the value of currencies is guaranteed
neither by states nor by gold reserves but by market mechanisms alone.[8] In
1972, spot transactions on the Chicago Mercantile Exchange were supplemented by an international money market for foreign currency futures,
and within the next three decades, trade with financial derivatives, which
either had not existed before 1970 or had existed only under exceptional
circumstances, had grown to become the world's biggest market. From an
annual value of only a few million dollars at the beginning of the 1970s,
its volume climbed to a thousand million by 1990 and rose to around

a hundred billion dollars by the turn of the millennium, roughly three times the value of worldwide consumer goods turnover.[9] Representatives of the new finance economy spoke of a "derivatives revolution" when referring to practices such as forward transactions with shares, securities, and mortgages. On the one hand, this meant expanding trade into previously untapped markets and exploiting less commonly traded assets with a view to integrating all possible financial sectors. Stockbroking became the standard for the finance economy, while the financial market itself became the market of all markets and the model for all market activities. On the other hand, this amounted to an apotheosis of the principle of risk transfer: price risks would be covered by spreading the risk further; speculative trade would be covered by more speculative trade. The explosion in the market for financial derivatives thus offered more than just the renewed prospect of realizing a "self-regulating" system. With its characteristic "magic," the derivatives market also opened up the prospect of achieving the kind of stability that had once been seen to depend on backing from precious metals and the gold standard or on exorbitant interventions by the state. This was now seen as achievable—indeed, optimally so—by means of "private transactions."[10] What the link between credit money and commodity money had once promised would finally be delivered by free foreign exchange and derivative markets.

Dealing in futures

In this system, which began operating in the 1980s, old ideas of equilibrium were linked to the current economic situation with the help of new financial instruments. The various components that can be distinguished within this system combined to form new commercial routines that have remained in place to this day. In the genealogy of today's finance and credit economy, forward transactions or futures took on a central, structuring function. They must be seen as perfect capitalist inventions and as expressions of a fundamental principle in capital transactions. As old as capitalism itself, they reveal an affinity for the future to be the motive force driving the relentless development of new financial products. On the one hand, the mechanism of futures trading is very simple and indeed had long been a fixture of stock market transactions: it is a contract to buy or sell a specified asset at a future date for a fixed price, a contract which therefore obliges both parties to accept whatever profits or losses may accrue in the interim. As early as the seventeenth century, several variants—options, option dealings, futures contracts—were described as standard practice on the Amsterdam stock exchange and addressed as problematic "time bargains" or "wind trade."[11] Such contracts were agreements between traders stipulating the obligation (in the case of forward commodities) or the right (in the case of options) to buy or sell for a fixed price at—or before—a future point in time.

On the other hand, the history of futures trading shows that time deals have been uncoupled from the exchange of goods in a way that is far from trivial. Futures trading on the stock exchange was continually attended by misgivings; it was limited by law or prohibited, for example, by decisions of the United States Supreme Court in 1889 or the German Reichstag in 1896. There was considerable concern about the difficulty of distinguishing between "real" and "fictitious" economic transactions. A futures contract seemed justified only if it was followed by actual delivery of the goods or underlying assets in question—a demarcation that was supposed to stop genuine trade from gradually sliding, via speculation, into mere gambling. Repeated attempts at temporary expedients have made it blatantly obvious, however, that such artfully drawn distinctions have no basis in any logic immanent to futures themselves. Since futures trading is only carried out on condition that the very goods on which the value of a transaction depends are manifestly absent (in this respect differing from spot or cash transactions), it was felt that the whole operation should at least be guaranteed by an intention, on the part of the contracting parties, to hand over or take delivery of the goods being traded. In other words, a "real intent" or an "intention to deliver" should be apparent, regardless of how or even whether the relevant transfer actually eventuated.

With this kind of casuistry, which has characterized legal commentary and antispeculation laws since the nineteenth century, the boundaries provisionally drawn between real and unreal values, real and fictitious transactions became critical or obsolete; Pierre-Joseph Proudhon had already quite logically declared futures trading to be a necessary and unavoidable constituent of a capitalist economy, that is, an economy determined by competitive enterprise, supply and demand, price fluctuations, and profit margins.[12] And following the demise of the Bretton Woods Agreement, when forward transactions no longer concerned countable quantities, like grain harvests or head of cattle, but rather financial assets, such as foreign exchange or securities, there was ultimately no sure way to contain futures trading. In 1976, for example, the Chicago Mercantile Exchange made it possible to hedge interest earnings on eurodollars against exposure to currency risks. The novelty of this innovation was that interest rates are deliverable neither de facto nor de jure.[13] Derivatives of this kind made deviation from the notion of base asset substrates and transactions irreversible; it is therefore only logical that since the 1980s, more and more international exchange venues have declared real and prospective deliveries to be irrelevant to forward contracts. In point of fact, futures trading can only be described in terms of its underlying logic: it circumvents both the physical conditions of production and the material conditions of transfer and transportation. In futures trading, the link between commodities and prices, payment and real values is either relaxed or completely severed. As Max Weber wrote, here

A deal is struck over a set of goods that are not present, and often "in transit" somewhere, or often yet-to-be produced; and it takes place between a buyer who usually does not himself wish to "own" these goods (in any regular fashion) but who wishes—if possible before he receives them and pays for them—to pass them along for a profit, and a seller, who usually does not yet have those goods, usually has not produced them, but wishes to furnish them for some earnings of his own.[14]

In short, someone who does not have a commodity and neither expects nor wants it sells this commodity to someone who also neither expects nor wants it and never actually takes possession of it.

The dynamic of futures trading—the driving force and crux of the capitalist economy—thus depends on two central functional elements. The first of these is self-referential communication: prices refer not to goods and products but to prices themselves; prices for things that are not currently to hand are calculated on the basis of price forecasts for things that will not be to hand in future. Prices are paid with prices. Prices are thus themselves commodities, freed from the burdens and inconveniences that encumber material possession, and they may rightly be classified as self-referential market events. Analogous to the way speculative statements in philosophy negate finite phenomena, this kind of trade performs an economic and semiotic act that culminates, not in a representation of the world but in its de-presentation, its voiding of presence; it deals with the things of this world only on condition of their manifest absence or obliteration.[15] Just as monetary and exchange values have always functioned as universal levelers of the most heterogeneous goods and services imaginable, so financial derivatives now make it possible to compare, exchange, and homogenize all possible kinds of capital, be it capital for trade, production, or credit. In the market for financial derivatives such as forwards, futures, options, and swaps that has arisen since the 1980s, monetary surrogates have become second-order means of payment. As part of the money supply in circulation, they guarantee the highest degree of liquidity and complete or fulfill the logic of the modern capital and credit economy.[16]

A further consequence is the redefinition of the nature and extent of speculation. Where the criterion for distinguishing between real and imaginary value no longer applies, and where hedging (or trade with financial derivatives) requires investment in risk (and thus more trade with financial derivatives), not only does investment become indistinguishable from speculation but both gain a new lease of life as matching sides of one and the same operation. What was once known as speculation now no longer differs from its former antitheses, whether trade on the one hand or gambling and betting on the other. From the broader perspective of a history of semantics, speculation loses its specific distinguishing features and becomes synonymous with liquidity creation. In any case, speculation has now taken on the characteristics of an oxymoron, since speculators—the gamblers and profiteers who "speculate" on the risky difference between present and future prices—now appear to be those who avoid all hedging and thus all speculative trade. It follows logically that the speculator is by definition someone who does not speculate.[17] Speculation has become the norm in financial transactions.

Efficient markets

Futures trading thus presents a logical counterpart to the capital and credit economy. Financial derivatives are a form of money that exists independently of the commodities market and the circulation of cash. That is why the syntactic structure of the modern finance economy demands a procedure that links current payment or investment decisions to the expectation that further decisions are always to be reckoned with, and so holds out the prospect of mastering time (that is, contingent futures). Only if the uncertainty of future prices (for foreign currencies, securities, and so on) can be offset by assigning a price to uncertainty itself will futures trading have the power to maintain equilibrium, control time, and confirm the self-regulatory character of the financial system, thereby securing the desired outcome of self-sustaining stability. That is why, as early as the beginning of the twentieth century, models were developed to enable buyers and sellers to make decisions based on the statistical probability of future price movements on stock markets. And since the middle of the century, at the latest, the main intellectual challenge has been to find a formula that makes the transition from present futures to future presents both predictable and likely, transforming what lies in the future and therefore differs from the present into something that resembles the present.

We might even note a point of contact here—to put it somewhat grandiloquently—between deep historico-philosophical structures and questions of finance mathematics. From the perspective of a history of discourse, it comes as no surprise that the most prominent and influential attempts of this kind were formulated in the 1970s, directly coinciding with the political and economic horizon opened up by the end of the Bretton Woods Agreement. These attempts involved procedures for placing probability theory at the very heart of financial practice. A particularly instructive example is provided by the famous set of formulae developed by the mathematicians and economists Robert C. Merton, Fischer Black, and Myron Scholes between 1969 and 1973. These formulae, subsequently endorsed by the Nobel Economic Sciences Prize Committee, became a standard feature of financial transactions as well as a fixed element in the system we know today.

What was once credited as the scientific discovery of a momentous truth in finance economics—as significant for financial markets as Newtonian mechanics was for physics—bears on the problem mentioned above and therefore concerns the question of how risk in financial markets can be eliminated by means of derivatives and dynamic hedging. It involves creating projected products that allow the value of future returns to be converted into present value, thereby stabilizing the dynamic disequilibrium that results from a credit economy and fluctuating exchange rates. If the price of future risks can be converted into current payments then future uncertainty can be calculated and compensated for in the present. By considering pricing equations for a given class of financial derivatives—in this case, options—we can detect, in the efforts of Black, Scholes, and Merton, the exemplary fabrication of a theoretical or discursive object that combines mathematical formalization with the adoption of certain guiding ideas and hypotheses about the way financial markets function.

What analysts have repeatedly seen as one of the foundational scenes of modern finance owes its existence to the assumption—inherited from older equilibrium theorems—that capital markets will turn out, in the long run, to perform efficiently. The neoclassical interpretation of market mechanisms and competition that had been developed since the 1930s was now applied to the finance economy. According to this updated version of the "efficient market hypothesis," a capital market that is efficient in the long term is one where, under ideal competitive conditions, "all available information is freely accessible to everyone, no transaction costs are incurred and all market participants function simultaneously as price takers." In addition, "homogenous expectations" are presumed to be in effect, along with the associated equilibrium models. This means that market participants agree about "the implications of available information" affecting "current prices" and the "probable distribution of future prices for individual capital investments." Businesses make justified decisions about investment in production, and consumers can pick and choose from securities or company shares on the assumption "that the prices of securities *fully reflect* all available information." In concrete cases, this means that share or security prices perfectly express the conjectures that analysts, investors, or managers are making about future returns and profit outlooks. And this also means that here a communication system of second-order observers has been established. Only a market "in which prices fully reflect available information" can be deemed an efficient one.[18] "Efficiency" is thus not only a fetishized key term in financial market theory (and in the economic regime as such); its position in this theoretical construct is also supported by the full spectrum of ideas deriving from the term's history, which—as Pierre Legendre remarks—links the forces of Providence to a rational order in the idea of "effecting" or "effectuation" (*efficere*) and so draws attention to the doctrinal nature of the system.[19]

Random walk

The financial market is presented as a self-referential and therefore frictionless universe in which information generates prices, prices generate buying decisions, and these in turn generate more information, prices, and decisions. This efficient process is linked to another precondition, however, and it is this which determines the models used in modern finance economics. At issue is not just the assumption that financial markets enjoy an advantage over other market forms because they operate "continuously" and are characterized by transactions of constantly variable sums, flowing smoothly through purchases and sales of any number and size. Their efficiency has as a further corollary that a random, almost stochastic movement lies at the heart of such market activity. Thus, in the 1960s a dissertation dating from 1900 was rediscovered in which the mathematician Louis Bachelier, working under the supervision of Henri Poincaré, expressed the oscillation of stock market quotations in a mathematical formula modeled on molecular movement (such as Brownian motion). In his *Théorie de la spéculation*, consecutive changes in price are defined as independent of any linear sequence and determined by identically distributed random variables; and the sum total of speculative operations describes a movement that functions analogously to the spread or diffusion of particles in gaseous mixtures.[20] Not until the second half of the twentieth century did these reflections acquire a plausible discursive framework, enabling them to be fused with hypotheses about universally efficient finance markets. Since prices on such markets include all information that is relevant at any given time, any change in these prices can only be due to new (that is, unforeseen) items of information, requiring new (and unforeseen) decisions to be made. Provided that markets process all items of information instantaneously, the history of price movements contains no knowledge that could be useful for future investment decisions. Present-day knowledge cannot be directly translated into knowledge of future presents.

The course taken by prices between various points in time is the subject of probability calculations and stochastics. It resembles a "random walk," a nonlinear path made up of a succession of random steps. Random movements have become a feature of efficient markets, and the "random walk theory" is a necessary complement to the efficient market hypothesis. This means that where all market players are in equal possession of all information currently in circulation, every opportunity for profit will immediately be seized by one of the players. So long as each of these operations immediately finds expression in market prices, price variations themselves must appear unpredictable and hence aleatoric. In a rational market, all relevant information (i.e., price differences) is annulled as soon as it is exploited; and competition between interested parties seeking to maximize profit ensures that speculation in individual instances thwarts the speculative character of the system as a whole. Arbitrage abolishes the effects of arbitrage and leaves no room for over- and under-valuation. In the words of several Nobel Prize winners, the situation can be described as follows:

If intelligent people are constantly shopping around for good value, selling those stocks they think will turn out to be overvalued and buying those they expect are now undervalued, the result of this action by intelligent investors will be to have existing stock prices already have discounted in them an allowance for their future prospects. Hence, to the passive investor who does not himself search for under- or overvalued situations, there will be presented a pattern of stock prices that makes one stock about as good or bad as another. To that passive investor, chance would be as good a method of selection as anything else.[21]

Thus, on the one hand, the rationality or efficiency of financial markets invites us to see a similarity between betting on future share performances and a game played by a blindfolded chimpanzee throwing darts at the shares section of a newspaper; the more efficient the markets, the more random the oscillations. On the other hand, a kind of balance is produced even here, so that chance fluctuations cluster around an average value and ultimately follow the spread of normal distribution.

A formula

This is the point at which Merton, on the one hand, and Black and Scholes, on the other, made their first attempts to determine prices in financial options, formulating a general model not just for how trade with financial derivatives is structured but also for the balancing tendencies inherent in the entire system. In the first place, the following initial conditions should or must apply: profit-oriented players, efficient markets, equally distributed and universally accessible information, friction-free transactions, and finally, constant variations that correspond to the pattern of normal distribution. Beyond this, existing prices (for shares and credits, for example) must be used to calculate a pricing horizon that, starting out from a future present, can act as a motive for pricing a present future. The current price of an option or derivative is justified, then, if a possible future of the "underlying"—the technical term for the security that must be delivered when a derivative contract is executed—returns in that price. Only through an inversion of this kind can uncertain prospects be transformed into the probability of future presents; and only this replication of future developments can justify the expectation that the risks of fluctuating rates and prices can be hedged and counterbalanced by trading with those risks. This also provides the focal point of the solution proposed by Black, Scholes, and Merton. Whereas the current price of a security, its basic or issuing price, the rate of interest, and the maturity date or duration of an option can all be factored into calculations as more or less known quantities, what is precariously unknown when it comes to calculating option prices is the degree to which they may deviate, that is, the volatility of the underlying.

This defines the parameters of the famous differential equation that attempts to grasp stochastic processes by means of a formula for logarithmic normal distributions:

$$rD_{T} = \frac{\partial D_{T}}{\partial T}^{T} + rS \frac{\partial D_{T}}{\partial S}^{T} + \frac{1}{2} \sigma^2 S^2 \frac{\partial^2 D_{T}}{\partial S^2}$$

where

D_T = price of derivatives with the term remaining (T)

S = share price

T = term remaining

r = risk-free constant interest rate

σ = standard deviation of expected constant returns (volatility).

FIGURE 3 (a and b)   The Black-Scholes differential equation.

To simplify matters somewhat, the problematic quantity, the unknown future volatility (sigma), is calculated according to the price amplitudes and random movements of underlying values in comparable historical time periods. There is no need to guess the particular hits and misses that possible futures may hold in store; all that is required is to calculate the scope for variation within which these could occur. On the one hand, the price of an option or a derivative is now no longer assessed according to the rise or fall of the underlying, that is, according to the apparent evidence of price trends. On the other hand, an assumption is already built into the calculation that unpredictable future prices will behave like unpredictable prices in the past and that their variations will be similarly distributed. While we may not know what will happen, we can assume that what is unforeseen (and indeed unforeseeable) will at least fall within the range of current expectations.[22]

There is no suggestion that specific prognoses can be made, only that future distribution patterns can be predicted. Ultimately, the "Capital Asset Pricing Model" calculates the scope for potential risks along with their corresponding profit outlooks. It provides information not just about the compilation of portfolios but also, in particular, about calculating prices for financial derivatives and hence about making claims on claims. However original the formula developed by Black, Scholes, and Merton may have been, however much it may have been anticipated by isolated and half-forgotten attempts from around the turn of the century, and however much it may stand out from a range of contemporary endeavors,[23] the success of their mathematical procedure was guaranteed not least by the fact that it responded to the financial problematic of the 1970s by introducing a new element into the discourse that harmonized with the basic tenets of neoliberalism.

We can identify in this formula, then, a mathematical representation of current market logics, the processes of which were codified on the model of differential equations for heat conduction and diffusion in statistical mechanics. The "efficient market" and "random walk" hypotheses were both implanted into this mathematical procedure, which can be considered the starting point for a general methodology of price formation in financial derivatives and the cornerstone of a new "super perfect-market paradigm."[24] Moreover, earlier suspicions—concerning, for example, the precarious proximity between derivatives trading and gambling—were mathematically laid to rest here; the invention of new financial products and the function of derivatives markets were mathematically legitimized. Investments in unknown future events became subject to strict calculation. At the same time, the Black-Scholes formula and its variants must be recognized as purely theoretical constructs, a kind of "enacted theory." This is where their performative aspect comes to the fore. Through this calculus, financial derivatives actually create their own conditions of possibility, appealing to the market to make their claim to economic rationality come true. In this respect, there has been much talk of an adaptation of economic reality to economic theory and the gradual emergence of a special "Black-Scholes world" that did not yet exist in the 1970s: not just a prognosis of market events but the establishment of protocols by which markets themselves could subsequently operate.[25] As a product of the new theoretical discourse, the formula mounts a compelling case for derivatives trading, thereby holding out the prospect of stabilizing the system and justifying its own theoretical implications.

Information

This circular process points to a further component that still influences the way the finance economy operates today. Thanks to the Black-Scholes formula and its variants, financial derivatives have not only become objects of mathematical formalization; they have also become specific media-technology formats. It is not by chance that the worldwide expansion in derivatives trading has coincided with the different stages of computing history and the development of information technology. Financial markets have always been structured by the close connection between price formation on stock exchanges and innovations in media technology, which since the nineteenth century have included the introduction of the telegraph, the use of transatlantic cables, and the accelerated communication of market information via ticker tape. To take only the example of the optical telegraph invented by Claude Chappe, we can see how the trend linking financial affairs to information technology spread like a virus across postrevolutionary France. In 1836, two Bordeaux bankers bribed a telegraph employee to allow additional signals to be added to official dispatches in the course of optical transmission. This system made it possible for them to gain a commercial advantage over their rivals by receiving information about price movements on French government bonds before letters or newspapers had arrived. This misuse of state news channels over a two-year period provides early evidence for how time differences can be systematically exploited and prices transformed in line with available information.[26]

The infrastructure of the modern finance economy was similarly defined by electronic and digital technologies. From the first plans to set up electronic financial markets in the 1960s, via the creation of computer-assisted stock exchanges, the provision of electronic trading systems and share platforms, to online brokering and the opening of the World Wide Web for stock market and financial transactions in 1993, advances in information processing and telecommunications have helped create the financial machinery that now determines a significant part of the world's social welfare.[27] This machinery is as essential for trading with financial derivatives as it is effective. The set formulae of the Black-Scholes model practically cry out for implementation by information technology. At first, option pricing was calculated by computer according to the Black-Scholes formula. Rather inconveniently, the relevant tables were then sold in print format to interested traders and subscribers.

As early as 1974, Texas Instruments manufactured a pocket calculator that was programmed with the relevant valuation formula and offered

X	UNITED STATES STL CORP	EXPIRATION	ANN INT	ANN DEV	DIV ANT	EX DATE	AMEX X	2 OF 7
		JLY 16 76	5.650%	21.00%	5.4700	8/ 3/75		
		OCT 15 76	6.230%	21.00%	5.4700	11/ 3/76		
		JAN 21 77	6.630%	21.00%				

	06/04/76			06/11/76			06/18/76			06/25/76			07/02/76		
	JLY 76	OCT 76	JAN 77	JLY 76	OCT 76	JAN 77	JLY 76	OCT 76	JAN 77	JLY 76	OCT 76	JAN 77	JLY 76	OCT 76	JAN 77

FIGURE 4   One of the tables generated by Fischer Black. The figures on the far left indicate the market prices; the next row represents the strike- or base-prices (i.e., the prices fixed at the close of an option agreement, when the relevant securities can be handed over to the buyer). The large numbers in the body of the table give the values for call options with a fixed maturity date (e.g., July 16, 1976) on the Fridays of successive weeks (e.g., June 4, 1976); the smaller figures give the amount that an option contract will vary by if the market price shifts by a dollar. The data in the table's headlines state the interest rate, Black's assumption about market volatility, and details about dividends (adapted from MacKenzie, *An Engine, Not a Camera*, 160).

Black-Scholes results for day trading. And a highly effective fusion of finance theory, mathematics, and information technology has been evident, at the latest, since the emergence of computerized trade in options and futures markets in the 1980s. To the extent that the efficient market hypothesis requires the efficient processing of information, an imitation of theory by economic reality can be noted here: "The more efficient capital transactions and financial markets become in the real world, the more exact become the continuous-time model's predictions about actual financial prices, products and arrangements. This means, in short, that reality will eventually imitate theory."[28] This market could only have been set up under new technological conditions. Financial theory, mathematization, and technical implementation enter into a productive interrelationship, such that the invention of new financial instruments and the installation of corresponding markets confirm each other in their raison d'être. The alliance of theory and technology holds out the prospect of combining maximum liquidity, optimal price determination, and efficient data transmission in consolidated financial markets. The dovetailing of finance mathematics and media technology ultimately legitimized talk of a "Midas formula"[29] that translates turbulence into predictable dynamics, and random market events into reliable profit outlooks.

The Black-Scholes model was declared the "most successful theory not only in the domain of finance, but also in the whole of economics."[30] This assessment is bound up with a number of basic assumptions, stratagems, and expectations about financial insights. If we look at the way the elements mentioned above—futures trading, new computational processes, and information technology—now interact in financial markets, we can see that a historical transformation has taken place. Information has replaced currency standards of various kinds as the basis for global finance. The credit economy and currency systems no longer depend for their stability on conversion into gold or commodity money; stability is conceived instead as an ongoing exchange between money and information. To the extent that prices on financial markets simultaneously compile information about the future of prices, information about money has become more important in transactions than money itself. The market installs an information-automatism. Efficient markets are markets for efficiently distributing information; competition now appears as competition for information. This extends all the way to today's competition in "high frequency trading," where the latest technologies provide an advantage of milliseconds when it comes to retrieving market information. If the international finance economy can be understood as a technologically implemented theory of money, then the circulation of money takes on the function of an information-producing apparatus. In this respect, it may be considered an essential aspect of what we now know as the information society.[31]

New oikodicy

Even as the new formula began remaking financial markets in its own image, its elegant simplicity and "beauty" drew frequent comment. Such judgments of taste undoubtedly derive from an essential, almost classical feature of the Black-Scholes model: it allowed the stabilizing forces of the market—and hence balancing and equilibrium effects—to reassert themselves. That is the much vaunted "Newtonianism" of the system. In a world of financial derivatives conceived along these lines, a compensation mechanism repays risks with returns and uncertainties with lucrative prospects. As Fischer Black once said, "the notion of equilibrium in the market for risky assets had great beauty for me. It implies that riskier securities must have higher expected returns, or investors will not hold on to them."[32]

Investors could now protect themselves against risk by "hedging" or spreading the risk; they could "rid themselves" of the risks attendant on investments and foreign currency—as envisaged by the Black-Scholes formula—by taking out option contracts tending in the opposite direction. It was a strategy that boded well for business: "The more we trade [with financial derivatives] the better off the society, because the less risk there is."[33] This Nobel Prize-winning conversion of guesswork into a science of finance also promised to amortize the effect of uncertain futures and thus the dimension of time in general. If we think in terms of normal distribution, mean values, and Gaussian or bell curves, we should be able to plot the pattern of variation for future events against the range of variations displayed by unpredictable events in the past. Future risks should behave analogously to existing risks. Accordingly, the commercial routines of financial markets are based on the premise that future expectations can be translated into expected futures and that, in the long run, homogeneity between the future present and the present future is more or less guaranteed to prevail.

Although uncertainties have not simply disappeared in this model, its dynamics suggest that the expansion and intensification of market activity will usher in a risk-neutral world, one in which an indeterminate future can be assimilated into the present since it is offset by determinable expectations about the future. The translation of economic data into integrable systems makes it possible to depict a world that moves gently and continuously from moment to moment, knowing neither crashes nor sudden leaps and bounds.

In such a world, the operational advantage of mathematical formalism corresponds with the theoretical presupposition that the system itself functions regularly, homogenously, steadily, and with an inherent tendency toward equilibrium. In this respect, the calculus devised by Merton, Black, and Scholes can be understood as a fully articulated allegory for the system as a whole, since—as the mathematician James Yorke once remarked—writing down the solution to a differential equation requires finding regular invariants and must therefore eliminate the possibility of discontinuity or chaos.[34] Any other "solution" would be disastrous for the status of economic theory as well as detrimental to its performative self-affirmation.

Despite drawing criticism from some quarters, the Black-Scholes model was accepted (with modifications) as a central functional element of the finance economy. As a result, the assumptions and viewpoints built into the liberal or neoliberal oikodicy—the balancing power of competition and price mechanisms—were implanted into everyday work processes and business routines. The model functions as a technologically implemented economic theory and could be understood as a model for risk management in general, as a political regulatory mechanism with universal applications. By articulating the vision that all events and relationships in the world around us can be assigned a market value—in a perfectly competitive world we only need to know the price of things—the new liberalism implied that a differentiated, quasi-molecular market can safeguard every possible future with securities, options, and derivatives and so reinstate a kind of earthly Providence. The conceptual framework of the finance industry could be used to "evaluate and price the risk in a wide array of applications, both financial and non-financial." These "option-like structures" are universalized in the face of "uncertain futures," holding out the utopian prospect of an all-encompassing, all-equalizing market.[35]

The new finance capitalism thus promises nothing less than a democratization of the financial world and a form of order which—equipped with concise theoretical models, optimized financial products, and digital technologies—will be better able to bring about social harmony than the utopian socialisms of the nineteenth century. That accounts for the visionary tone recently adopted in financial theory:

We need to democratize finance and bring the advantages enjoyed by the clients of Wall St. to the customers of Wal-mart. We need to extend finance system beyond our major financial capitals to the rest of the world. We need to extend the domain of finance beyond that of physical capital to human capital, and to cover the risks that really matter in our lives. Fortunately, the principles of financial management can now be expanded to include society as a whole. And if we are to thrive as a society, finance must be for all of us—in deep and fundamental ways.

Democratizing finance means effectively solving the problem of gratuitous economic inequality, that is, inequality that cannot be justified on rational grounds in terms of differences in effort or talent. Finance can thus be made to address a problem that has motivated utopian or socialistic thinkers for centuries. Indeed, financial thinking has been more rigorous than most other traditions on how to reduce random income disparities. Equipped with modern digital technology, we can now make these financial solutions a reality.[36]

End of history

The removal of limits on financial markets and the creation of "international markets for human capital"—underscored by a triumphalist rhetoric of expansion—envisaged a proactive, flexible adaptation of societies to situations of continuous risk exposure. In this we can detect a reform of the old welfare state and the emergence of a new format, a society that is not only based on competition but might also, with some justice, be termed a modular risk culture. This new social order knows neither class nor party, only the bonds of financial interest and economic partnership. The social field is now embedded in the dynamics of finance capitalism. On the one hand, this shift reminds us that, since Adam Smith, political economy has consistently been inspired by moral philosophy and that now, with the implementation of the latest financial techniques, a kind of practical reason also holds sway: like no other social invention before it, the intricate network of innovative financial products is said to ensure the realization of "distributive justice" across all life situations.[37]

On the other hand, we can clearly see how the claims made by older versions of theodicy are resuscitated in the core concepts of the new financial system. The assumed efficiency of financial markets entails that we can only imagine their relation to the world as the ongoing optimization of all relations within that world. This means that individual anomalies and crises cannot cast doubt on the benign functioning of the system as a whole: "It would be absurd to junk the system because of a few failures." And it also means that regrettable cases of "moral hazard," or misdirected speculation, are either ruled out in this system or attributed merely to the mishaps and misdeeds of individual agents.[38] Things may go awry from time to time, but the system itself continues to function as it should. From the perspective of this order, the future could only appear as infinitely foreseeable and consequently lacking in true futurity: with "risk-offsetting investments" and the ongoing exploitation of future risk, we enter into a kind of posthistorical condition in which it is no longer possible to discern any single line of historical development, only random and molecular movements. Such, at any rate, is the claim made by the equilibrium theorem in its most recent reformulation. In its current form, the theory envisages not just dynamic balance but an equalizing process that offsets the uncertainty of present futures with the predictability of future presents, thereby efficiently minimizing the power and influence of time on the course of events.

It is unsurprising, then, that financial thinking repeatedly and almost inevitably succumbs to the temptation to imagine an end to history. Thus Kevin Hassett, economist and one-time chief economic adviser to presidential candidate John McCain, bizarrely set out to prove that neither world wars nor economic crises, neither deportations nor mass murders, neither the Korean nor the Vietnam war had ever taken place on American financial markets; all they had ever witnessed were rising returns, and nothing but steadily increasing profits can be expected from them in the future, too.[39] And in the 1990s, the golden years of the new finance economy, rumor had it that thanks to flourishing financial markets, the drama of economic cycles was coming to a halt and "the end of economic history" itself had arrived. With information technologies and increasingly stable commercial operations, the United States, at least, would enter a state "beyond history."[40] Speculation and hedging were supposedly financing the way to a posthistorical epoch in which economic stabilization would contribute to social, political, and cultural stability. Such views were in keeping with philosophies intent on reconciling the old nation-states with the new economic and political liberalism and calling—with Francis Fukuyama—for the advent of the posthistorical world and an end to history in general.

Here too, the "liberal revolution in economic thought" cements the now fully established alliance between liberal democracy and the "free market"—and it is no accident that this "good news," these evangelical or glad tidings, date back to the "remarkable developments in the last quarter of the twentieth century."[41] Since the 1970s, the vanishing point of financial theory is to be found in the figure of a system that achieves stability by rendering its dynamic processes atemporal. The future is always already priced in. And in this respect, too, the liberal capitalist oikodicy reasserts itself, maintaining that Providence is still at work in the market. Yet this hope for an earthly Providence, unlike the philosophical theodicies of old, does not conclude with a Panglossian thought experiment; it culminates instead in a far-reaching, worldwide social experiment that has not yet come to an end.

Economic and Social Reproduction

Oikonomía

There can be no doubt that neoclassical financial and economic theory also operates with assumptions about stability and equilibrium models that can be called deterministic. The order of this oikodicy is characterized by a dynamic equilibrium in which atomized competition on financial markets initiates a circulation of risk, raising the prospect of balancing the uncertainty of present futures with the predictability of future presents. In this we can detect signs of what has recently been termed a "financialization," characterized by the prominence assigned to capital turnover and financial motives, by the influence of affiliated industries, instruments, players, and institutions, by the inclusion of ever-new participants, by the ever-expanding volume of financial products and their returns, and by the privileged status accorded to financial markets as such. This horizon spans a system of mutual obligations in which the temporal structure of financial contracts sets the standard for all contractual agreements and for social cohesion itself. The figure of a new *contrat social* comes into play.[1] With that, and at the same time, a dynamic is established which takes the reproduction of finance capital—the dominance of its rhythms, cycles, and mechanisms—as the model for all other economic, social, and cultural forms of reproduction. At any rate, the new oikodicy, along with the relations, event types, and forms of interaction it sets up, promises to provide a blueprint for codifying the social bond.

In this enterprise we can recognize a problematic which, if it is to be adequately described and theoretically conceptualized, bids us revisit older scenes of political thought. We would do well to recall the prehistory of this discussion of an economic fatalism that sees society and the economy as being determined by the same laws of production. The famous reflections in Book One of Aristotle's *Politics* on the purposeful order of the *pólis*, on the role of *oikonomía*, the acquisition of exchange goods and the function of money, may be seen to contribute to an art of discrimination that gauges the fate of the polity by the mechanisms it puts in place to maintain and perpetuate its internal structures. At issue here is not just the notorious and influential exclusion of the monetary economy, or "chrematistics," from the realm of the political, which was to resonate far beyond Scholasticism all the way into modern political economy. More precisely, Aristotle is concerned with demonstrating how a particular distinction or delimitation quite directly affects the form taken by diverging modes of reproduction.

How the natural order of the *pólis* is constituted in Aristotle is sufficiently known. Here, living in a community—communal involvement or *koinōnía politikḗ*—is initially realized in the *oíkos* or household, whereas the life of the combined households is realized in their working towards the goals of political life, *autárkeia* and *eudaimonía*, the self-sufficient and good or fulfilled life of the *pólis*. With that, the political bond is not only declared the origin or goal (*télos*) of every social form; it is not just regarded as the end point of a movement by which the parts come together to form a political whole (*sýntheton*) and, in so doing, accord with their natural (or teleological) constitution. This political teleology further entails that the business of domestic life—economics or *oikonomía*, together with the related activities of making a living, acquiring goods, and providing for the household—is subordinated to political ends and remains embedded in the form of commonality. *Oikonomía* is necessarily a function of *politikḗ* or it has no existence at all. For the Aristotelian *zṓon politikón* there is therefore an "oikonomic" activity only to the extent that nature—and hence the goals immanent to the political bond—reproduces itself in and through such activity. The political animal is economic only insofar as it is political.[2] And what figures here as the economy proves to have no independent existence, as has frequently been noted of "premodern" economic modes; it has no laws and mechanisms of its own and fits seamlessly into the conditions for maintaining the sociopolitical status quo.

Against this background, however, the course taken by the Aristotelian analysis of *oikonomía* is no less predictable than it is precarious. For just as individual households (*oikía*) figure as purposeful parts of the *polís*, and the practices of *oikonomía* in turn as an element of politics, so an analogous configuration of parts and whole can be detected in *oikonomía* itself, which likewise betrays a teleological orientation. Accordingly, not only are sovereign, conjugal, and paternal relations (*despotikē̂, gamikē̂, patrikē̂*) identified as parts of *oikonomía*; above all, the question arises as to how the art of acquiring exchange goods—and with it the aspects of trade (*metablētikē̂*) and moneymaking (*chrēmatistikē̂*)—stands in relation to household management and its goals. Are these activities intrinsic to *oikonomía* from the outset, are they constitutive parts of it, or are they merely subordinate elements?

This is the point at which Aristotle's argument departs dramatically from its previous course. On the one hand, we can only speak of a natural commerce which, as part of the whole, conforms to the nature of *oikonomía*, and hence the *polís*, if it relates to that "true wealth" which finds its limit in the elimination of want, in needs-based use and consumption, and which respects the "amount of such property sufficient in itself for a good life." As a purposeful part of economics or politics, acquired property (*ktēsis*) is exhausted through use. Just as every means finds its natural limit in the end (only ends themselves can be limitless), so all external goods receive their inherent limitation in "oikonomic" or domestic use. They fulfill their purpose in providing the material basis for a good life or for life as such, and in the process they succumb to the law of their own finitude. Correlative to this are a specific exchange type and a specific way of using money: to the extent that all exchange acts are extinguished in the elimination of want and the guarantee of a self-sufficient life, and to the extent, moreover, that they qualify as a fair exchange, one involving an appropriate distribution of goods and respecting the bond of reciprocity, such transactions may still rightly be deemed purposeful or natural. Human needs, and mutual exchange oriented towards such needs, constitute, support, and promote the political bond.[3] That ultimately signifies the prevalence of a cyclical conception of time, which—in accordance with the Anaximander fragment—is distinguished by its periodic return, by the circle of acquiring and using, becoming and decay. The communal bond of the *polís* reproduces itself in the sublunary cycle of nature.

Chrematistics

On the other hand, however, it is precisely here, in his analysis of economic practices (including the art of acquiring exchange goods), that Aristotle identifies a teleological confusion that divides what belongs together and dissociates what is the same, bringing about a critical deviation or aberration in the orderly series of goals. At this point, a fundamental difference is introduced which sets "oikonomic" activity at odds with its primary or natural tendency. For according to Aristotle, we can recognize, in the divergence of exchange acts and money, not just a reaction to an expansion of the community and to a spatial extension of trade; and these do not just bring about a temporary interruption in the closed circle of *autárkeia*, a provisional hiatus between acquisition and use. Rather, Aristotle's canonic argument is that precisely the intervention of the monetary function sets off a ruinous escalation, making possible an "other kind" (*eídos*) of exchange practice, the distorted mirror image or double of the first.

While this enterprise, designated commercial exchange or retail trade (*kapēlikē*)—a rich source of characters for Aristophanean comedy—is still located in the *polís* and grounded in the bond of commonality, it has the effect of making movable goods and possessions oddly unlike themselves. A shoe, for example, can be used for walking in and also as a means of exchange; in the second case, however, it departs from the end for which it was made and ultimately finds a distorted realization in the institution of money (*nomisma*). Even if the use of means of exchange—be they shoes, metals, or stamped coins—is not "unnatural" in itself, the critical point is that they make it possible for the same item to be used in two radically different yet interchangeable ways. Such goods may be acquired, firstly, in order to be used, but they may also, secondly, be traded for profit. In the means of exchange—in money—a reversal of means and ends is made possible; the means is convertible into the end, the instrument into the work. External goods are acquired not just in order to be used, but also for the purpose of acquiring other external goods, hence in order to increase the turnover of means of exchange or money. Here the shoe is no longer a shoe; and here a precarious change of form takes place, a deviation that might also be called *parekbasis*, a digression from the right and natural path. Intrinsic to the means is its perversion into an end in itself, and hence a deceptiveness which, in one and the same operation, makes one type of exchange (pursued for the satisfaction of needs) indistinguishable from another (pursued for the sake of profit).

This very indeterminacy of two separate types of exchange is what determines the fate of politics. For this is the characteristic digression or aberration that occurs in moneymaking (*chrēmatistikē*): here the acquisition of exchange goods no longer finds its limit in need or use; instead, it is redirected to an inner limitlessness in which the purposeful expenditure of means aims at an increase in means.[4] With the pursuit of moneymaking, no limits are set to the investment of means, and hence to commercial enterprise. Chrematistics is limitless with respect to both means and ends, and is thus defined by its inner boundlessness. The unity of the exchange relation is breached; in chrematistics, "oikonomic" activity is haunted or travestied by a fatal doppelganger. This unnatural turn of events, however, arises from the natural development of things, a mix-up or teleological confusion that is documented, in Book One of the *Politics*, in the ambivalent and shifting semantics of the concept *chrēmatistikē*. Whereas initially, in the third chapter, the term designates the art of acquiring exchange goods in general, conceived as part of *oikonomía*, and hence the procurement of life's necessities (*chrēmata*), later, in the central ninth chapter, it is used in its "authentic" sense for the special case of moneymaking or the profit-driven acquisition of goods, which contradicts the nature of *oikonomía*. Finally, in the tenth chapter, it once again refers to the art of acquiring exchange goods as such. This is a significant oscillation that makes the character of chrematistics appear in a contradictory—at once natural and unnatural—light.[5]

Dark entelechy

This not so much historical as logico-genetical development, leading from the procurement of movable goods via barter to the monetary economy, is not just presented by Aristotle in strict analogy to the development of the political bond, from *koinōnía* via *oíkos* to *polís*; rather, it culminates in a volte-face and places political ontology on its head. And in the function of money, in the replacement of unlimited goals by limitless means, chrematistics assumes the form of a perverted or dark entelechy. When Aristotle subsequently describes such boundlessness as manifestly unnatural (*parà phýsis*), what he has in mind is, in the first place, a departure from the series of political goals, a rejection of communal involvement and a depoliticization of the political bond. The proportions of commonality grow indistinct. For with the limitless striving implied in chrematistics—which, incidentally, runs directly counter to the Aristotelian concept of striving—reciprocal involvement in human affairs is no longer directed towards the satisfaction of mutual needs and the common good of a fulfilled life. Instead, it is now driven by the prospect of each participant gaining goods without end. Accordingly, the *Ethics* of Aristotle is not content to trace back "the drive for profit" and "insatiable desire" to particular and local vices, such as lack of restraint, cowardice, or anger, but conceives them as "injustice" per se, that is, as an attack on the law of appropriate involvement or reciprocity. Chrematistics explodes the format of mercantile justice; it undermines the grounding of the commonwealth in natural law; it decenters the bond of *koinōnía*, otherwise fixed on the middle (*méson*) and the relative suitability of all means. And it opens up the path of a perpetually unequal exchange that veers from the high road of justice and the law, leading to a realm where the perfection of the political animal comes face to face with its "worst"—and that also means tyrannical—possibilities.[6] The symbolic bond of the exchange relation takes a diabolical turn.

Above all, however, the development of chrematistics touches on a dimension in which we may discern the collapse of the natural order as such, and with it a break in the onto-cosmological circle. At the climax of the chrematistic escalation, we encounter a kind of artificial procreation which, in the moneymaking business or usury, in the lending out of money for profit (*obolostatikē*), spawns a self-reproducing means, a "breed" or "offspring" or simply "interest" (*tókos*), which makes it possible for money to father itself, so to speak, to proliferate and flourish by its own devices. In a similar vein, Plato had already spoken of interest as the "the

progeny (*tókoi*) of the parent sum." Indeed, the spontaneous movement of
this extreme form, according to Aristotle, can no longer be reconnected
to the logic of the simple exchange or purchase. The route back to the
natural order of *oikonomía* and *polís* has been cut off. Instead, in the business of moneymaking, money gives birth to more money, "and this is the
explanation of the name (*tokós*), which means the breeding of money. For
as offspring resemble their parents, so usury is money bred of money."[7]

We are dealing here, then, with a monstrous filiation, one that
necessarily characterizes the "most unnatural" way in which exchange
goods are acquired, denatures nature itself, and promotes the limitless
self-reproduction of means. The circle of acquisition and need has been
ruptured once and for all; an unnatural form of procreation has entered
into creative rivalry with the natural order and its reproductive cycles, and
this form will ultimately dictate its own temporal regime. For if chrematistics has a tendency to expand into the infinite and unbounded (*ápeiron*),
if money propagates itself in endless progression, then time is no longer
subordinate to the cardinal points staked out by the periodic movements,
the cycles of *phýsis*, the coming into being and dying away of all things.
Time is out of joint, suspended and deflected from its original trajectory.
A temporality governed by need is replaced by an open and linear time
in which the power of the future is made manifest: an imperfect (*atelés*),
abstract, and exterior time of nonrecurring times.

The conversion of time into the procreative force of the monetary
form amounts to a subversion of natural temporality, giving rise to an
autonomous and empty form of time, measurable and "mintable," a time
without characteristics and devoid of any particular quality: "Chrematistic trade is an exchange which seems to put a price tag on time, since it
essentially consists of an exchange between different points in time."[8] In
the accrual of interest, time—as the index of sheer passing—has become
money. If we are justified in speaking here of "money time" or "capital
time," then this is also a deregulated time, brought into being by the very
teleological aberration that plunges the same into an abyss of difference
and produces the "specter" of "what does not come back to itself."[9] That
is the vanishing point of the confusion recounted, in all its drama, in
Book One of the Aristotelian *Politics*: in the boundless proliferation of
money and its offspring, a spectral double or travesty of the natural order

is invoked; an erratic movement is unleashed that perverts the internal dynamic driving the growth and preservation of the political organism.

Nameless business

While it would be wrong to identify the Aristotelian analyses of economics, exchange, and monetary form as a precursor to modern political economy, they can nonetheless be credited with having introduced a productive, apt, and conceptually nuanced distinction that serves, not least, to juxtapose diverse materialities in the production and reproduction of the communal bond. The "natural" self-perpetuation of the political organism stands opposed to the "artificial" breeding of money. Chrematistic processes manifest aspects of a dispersal or disaffiliation which releases them from the architecture of economics and politics. In developing their own dynamic, they unleash a disintegrative force that assails the political life form from without or undermines it from within. The "aberrant" use of money thus raises the specter of the ruin of the *polís* and its communal form, and it reminds us that the Aristotelian *Politics* is contemporaneous with the downfall of the Attic commonwealth in the fourth century. The philosopher of the *polís* steps on stage as the curtain falls; his entry coincides with the deterritorialization of the political terrain.

We may further perceive, in this analysis of chrematistics, the resonance of a gradual consolidation of market activity and long-distance or maritime trade (*emporía*) in the environs of the ancient city-states. Whereas the Homeric epics did without a word for trade, at most designating in *prēktéres* a free agent, fixer, or dealer, with overtones of piratical entrepreneurship, and whereas Plato still advised that cities be established not on the coast but eighty stadia from the sea, so as to keep the unreliable, promiscuous trafficking of trade centers at a safe distance, from the fourth century onwards we see signs of a burgeoning mercantile trade—as in the Attic *agorá*—as well as concessions and legal guarantees granted to foreign traders (*díkē emporikē*). The Aristotelian analysis of chrematistics is thus marked by a certain perplexity towards the disconcerting novelty of commercial practices and the institutional crisis they helped precipitate—here too a reminder that trading on a commercial scale can by no means be understood as a gradual evolution from local and time-honored economic modes.[10]

This finding may be generalized. Just as, according to Benveniste, there are no common words to designate trade and traders in the Indo-European languages, such forms of enterprise evidently lying outside all occupations, practices, and techniques and being characterized as mere "busy-ness" (as in the Latin *neg-otium*, the sheer "absence of leisure"), so economic history tells us that markets in the commercial sense first arose on the outskirts of cities, often in connection with military campaigns, with invasions or pillaging raids and the risky undertakings these entailed.[11] At any rate, there is no evidence to suggest—as modern economic legend would have it—that commercial practices, market relations, and mercantile mentalities grew organically, as it were, from needs-based economic modes. Local economies were characterized by an absence of market economies and market-economic relationship networks, and the development of such networks, until well into the Middle Ages, went hand in hand with their detachment from political communities. Commercial enterprise was both unattached and foreign, in every sense of the word.

A fracture line thus appeared in Aristotle's investigations along which, over the subsequent course of Western cultural and discursive history, there repeatedly arose the question as to whether, how, and with what consequences the laws of economic and market-driven reproduction interfere with the laws governing the self-preservation of political and social bodies. Since Scholasticism, for example, the time of chrematistics has competed with the time of creation, God's special property, acquiring a taint of blasphemy on account of its stubborn secularity and artificial progeny. And however tortuous and complex the relationship between Old Europe's bans on usury and the need for capital may have been, however porous the boundaries between Christendom and market processes may actually appear—it was from tensions of this kind, and not least from a theological transcription of Aristotelianism, that there emerged a striking array of figures which, as outcast, sinful, parasitic, or simply spectral personifications, were made to embody the precarious status accorded the monetary economy, investment capital, and the charging of interest on loans. To the spectrum of a trifunctional society consisting of clergy, peasantry, and military (or nobility), which Georges Dumézil and Georges Duby have demonstrated for medieval Europe, there was added another, fourth species which, as one contemporary preacher put it, stands aloof from the community and the "labor of men."[12] It is a counterpart to autochthony. Its diverse variations, ranging from the leprous usurer of the Middle Ages to the anti-Semitic denunciation of "Jewish" finance capitalism, do not just rehearse the notorious stigma of the alien, the placeless, or the proscribed. They also demonstrate a sustained engagement with fertility semantics, reflecting in the process the reproductive accomplishments of Western societies.

Money and fertility

Against this background, we can make out two complementary lines of development or historical traces which diverge, converge, or intersect at numerous points. On one side, the artificial births, travesties of creation, and reproductive acts engendered, *contra naturam*, by liquid capital all stand for an industrious infertility which condemned the usurer to a place alongside the sodomite in Dante's Hell, for example, or reappeared in the form of Shylock's sterile ducats in Shakespeare's *Merchant of Venice*.[13] On the other side, and conversely, money's infinite fecundity could become, from the Early Modern age onwards, a figure for the potency of productive forces in general. For example, a bottomless moneybag that appears in one of the first German novels in prose, *Fortunatus* (1509), not only generates a series of picaresque adventures for the protagonist, and hence a novelistic narrative as such. Above all, what is so special about this moneybag is that its wealth is directly sexualized and associated with quite specific ideas about reproduction: according to this text, probably written in the trading centers of Augsburg or Nuremberg, the stream of money will never run dry so long as it is diverted once a year to provide a dowry for a virgin without means, thereby enabling her to wed and bear children. The fortunate owner of the "lucky purse" (*Glückseckel*) must further see to it that his own family line is carried on—a striking affiliation of the biblical injunction to "go forth and multiply," genealogical duration, and liquid capital. Money's associative quality has transformed the Aristotelian (or Scholastic) disjunction of money *or* life into a conjunction of money *and* life, directly linking the proliferation of life to the potency of wealth.[14] And it is not surprising in the end that this coupling of fertility and finance was to become, some two hundred and fifty years later, in one of the most famous documents of a new mercantile reason, a manifesto for economic vitality and its procreative power. In its second appearance in Benjamin Franklin's *Advice to a Young Tradesman*—a prominent reference text for Max Weber's account of the "spirit of capitalism"—the manifesto reads:

Remember, that money is of the prolific, generating nature. Money can beget money, and its offspring can beget more, and so on. Five shillings turned is six, turned again it is seven and three-pence, and so on till it become an hundred pounds. The more there is of it, the more it produces every turning, so that the profits rise quicker and quicker. He that kills a breeding sow, destroys all her offspring to the thousandth generation. He that murders a crown, destroys all that it might have produced, even scores of pounds.[15]

In these examples, the coupling of fecundity and money has taken on an almost dynastic quality: what in Franklin's "crown" still survives as an association with sovereign authority was illustrated in *Fortunatus* with the quasi-regal insignia of the prolific moneybag.

These two lines of development could be pursued further. We could document, for example, how in the nineteenth century—the age of bio-politics and accumulated industrial and finance capital—the discursive fracture lines mentioned above branch off and cross over, how they find a focal point in the idea of "life," how they release forces of attraction and repulsion, and not least, how they give rise to numerous model narratives which position themselves as so many variants of a "critique of political economy." We might think here of Balzac's story *Gobseck* (1830), in which a landless, sexless, and unattached allegorical figure for capital ultimately forms new alliances, establishes himself with an *ergo sum papa* as the paternal origin of both familial and financial genealogies, and in this way bequeaths a doubly fruitful inheritance; or of Gustav Freytag's novel *Debit and Credit* (*Soll und Haben*, 1855), where parasitical Jewish credit dissolves and corrupts all idyllic relations and can only be banished or made to prosper through the benign influence of German capital, by German merchants on German soil, in German genealogies and German commercial practices—an ominous alliance of capital and race. We could think, too, of Émile Zola's stock market novel, *Money* (*L'Argent*, 1891), written against the background of a contemporary wave of bankruptcies, which pursues the project of recoding finance capital in conformity with

FIGURE 5   Frontispiece of *Fortunatus*, Augsburg 1509.

Catholicism and which circles around an enterprise that, following the example of the protagonist, draws parallels between speculative and sexual practices, professes its faith in social fertility and the élan vital, yet leaves behind only further bankruptcies and "degenerate" offspring in the end. The utterly dissimilar tendencies and plotlines of such narratives converge in one of the great problems preoccupying the nineteenth century: the question of how movements of money and capital flows come to be reterritorialized in the life of the social body, which psychosocial types and personifications emerge as a result, and how economic processes and social structures interpenetrate to produce diverse conflict situations, hybrids, affiliations, and resonance amplifications. The primacy of the capitalist economic form makes it necessary to work through the tensions arising from competing modes of reproduction. Nothing less than the dominant code of the social bond and its self-perpetuation is at stake.

"Filiative" capital

Such demarcations, boundary phenomena, and transvaluations help to inform us about the roundabout ways in which Western societies responded to the dynamics of market activity and the capitalist economy. They indicate ways of repudiating, or adapting to, diverse birth scenes of capitalism; and the varying degrees of distance or proximity which they articulate attest to critical interferences between social or political reproductive cycles and vital economic processes. While it would be impossible to subsume the history of the unleashing of economic forces in the West under a continuous evolutionary process or under a single concept of capitalism, we can nonetheless identify an astonishingly resilient elemental kernel that the various different "capitalisms"—from the emergence of commercial markets via mercantile capitalism to industrial and finance capitalism—all have in common. This kernel may assume greater definitional consistency when viewed against the background of the discursive situation that has just been outlined.

However we choose to define the various "spirits" of capitalism—as the rational calibration of irrational drives; as the separation of the means of production from labor-power; as a market economy organized by and for private interests; as the dominance of a dynamic entrepreneurial class; as the unlimited accumulation of capital through formally peaceful means—in the spectrum of the countless attempts at definition we can detect a more or less constant problematic. According to this problematic, the question of "capitalism" or the question of the capitalist form always implies two things. It assumes, firstly, that the processes of modern economic modes cannot simply be reduced to the dynamism of a closed subsystem operating in concert with other social subsystems. And it points, secondly, to those arenas in which social reproduction in general appears to be inextricably intertwined with the self-reproduction of capital and of market mechanisms, in particular. If it is true that the development of modern political economy is bound up with the end of Old European economics, then the chrematistics of old acquires a new and privileged discursive space. We may speak of a capitalist economy wherever the "artificial" or chrematistic reproduction of forms of capital, including their internal dynamics and crises, has become the key criterion for social vitality. Capitalism would thus not be a homogeneous system but a particular way of organizing the relationship between economic processes, social order, and technologies of government in accordance with the mechanisms of capital reproduction.

This resonates with a Marxist intuition. Hence we can—following Marx's analyses—only speak of capitalist modes of production if we presuppose a "filiative" form of capital. In this form, commercial and finance capital no longer stand in loose connection to, or enter into strategic partnership with, nonaffiliated, non-economic modes of production (as in the various Early Modern alliances between trading houses and the feudal system). Instead the question arises as to how the dissolution of all possible forms of property into capital flows, on the one hand, and the transformation of all imaginable activities and modes of production into "abstract labor," on the other, are recombined or "affiliated" on a new level. Only under this condition can the self-reproduction of capital be grasped as the dominant machine which appropriates all productive forces and productions for itself and installs itself as the new "quasi-cause," the coordinate for the self-preservation of the social and political bond. Capital has assumed responsibility for producing all "filiative" relationships.[16] In this form of capital, furthermore, the difference between the two functions of money—to mediate between exchange and use values, on the one hand, and to circulate as surplus value in bank notes and credit (i.e., to provide an investment stream), on the other—has become unrecognizable. In the "interminable movement" Money–Commodity–Money, the social conditions for the production of surplus value vanish from the self-representation of capital; value has "acquired the occult quality of being able to add value to itself. It brings forth living offspring, or, at the least, lays golden eggs."[17] The movement of capital appears here as a self-generating life form that subordinates the social conditions of its existence to its own logic. Precisely because the social field is represented in capital through its lack of representation, it becomes subject to the laws of capital.

That is why, according to Marx, conditions of production need to be understood as conditions of reproduction. The "filiative" qualities of capital imply that capitalist production "of itself" incessantly reproduces the "separation between labor-power and the means of labor," the opposition between the forces of labor and the means of production, and hence its own "conditions of exploitation": "The capitalist process of production, therefore, seen as a total, connected process, i.e. a process of reproduction, produces not only commodities, not only surplus value, but it also produces and reproduces the capital-relation itself; on the one hand the capitalist, on the other the wage-laborer."[18] However antiquated such terminology may appear from the vantage point of our own, "postindustrial" capitalism, one thing cannot be denied: more than anyone else, Marx found a way to reconnect with the Aristotelian theory design under new premises, posing, alongside the question of the logic of economic processes, the question of the place and status of a productive and self-(re)producing human form. From this perspective, a stringent "critique of political economy" would not only have to do away with the aporias admitted into the classical theories of economics; nor need it just be understood as a flagrant procedure for unmasking the estrangement processes encrypted in the value form, or for confronting the specter of exchange value and the metamorphosis of commodities with a critical ontology. It would have to begin, above all, by coming to terms with a formation which, as "capitalist," is characterized by the fact that each and every one of its economic productions reproduces a specific division of the social field. The self-perpetuation of the capitalist form has become a *fait social total*.

Vital politics

In some respects, several of the various "neoclassical" or "neoliberal" schools took these lessons to heart, radicalizing the orientation of political economy in recent times. Since the midtwentieth century, at the latest, one question in particular has moved to the forefront of attention: how is it possible to uphold the parameter conditions under which market laws and the laws of capitalist economics will be able to harmonize with the laws governing the reproduction of society? Market laws, it is suggested, are not necessarily restricted to market phenomena; nothing less than an "economics of the social body, modeled on the principles of a market economy," is envisaged. The principles of an optimized social productivity presuppose a heightened need for integration into economic relationship networks. In general terms, it is a question here of establishing a form of governance in which vital social processes are dictated by economic dynamics. This not only means restructuring institutions with that end in mind, developing an axiomatics whose formal (legal and institutional) frameworks guarantee that social order will be constituted according to market-economic mechanisms and that a space for the survival of capitalism will be created. Rather, market relations are to be interpreted expansively. They now extend to cover all relations and interactions, the "total field of human action" or a general "praxeology."[19] While specific expectations of increased economic efficiency are invested in the synchronization of economic and social reproductions, so too are hopes for a social formation in which the revitalizing forces of a "nonalienating" capitalism will be fully realized. The alienating tendency assumed to be at work in capital is to be done away with.

In the course of such reflections, the contours of the older *homo economicus* are perceived, in all their limitations, as the profile of a "rational fool." On the one hand, "economic man" is now deanthropologized, driven out of the anthropological format that had defined him in the eighteenth and nineteenth centuries. More recent economic theory grasps the substrate of *homo economicus* no longer as a shifting amalgam of desires, inclinations, and interests, but as a mere abstraction, a fiction or model whose decision-making game is deployed for clarifying particular situations and problems. *Homo economicus* henceforth operates as a kind of theoretical probe or experimental procedure for testing and evaluating the functionality of institutions, organizations, and communication forms, for example. He has evolved from a more or less real entity into a heuristic figure, a role constructed solely for analyzing context-bound decision-making processes on a case-by-case basis.

On the other hand, and conversely, the non-economic remnant deducted from *homo economicus*, the "whole human being," now appears as a new productive factor in its own right. With the latest drive in innovation and in view of declining profit margins, hitherto untapped resources are opened up for development. The imperative of the new economy is to transcend the very limits of the economic by exploiting the capital(s) of the everyday world, the lifeworld, the world of interpersonal relationships. A kind of *Vitalpolitik* is called for, a "politics of life" per se,[20] which aims at harmonizing economic and social milieus and which sets its sights on individuals in their entirety, watching over them from morning to night, in their homes and in their beds, as lovers and as dreamers, in sickness and in health. The economy—or rather, capitalism—must constantly be realized anew. In a sense, it has undergone a makeover to make it appear compassionate, soulful, and meaningful; at any rate, it no longer cares to be mistaken for a rationalistic calculation of profits.

Economic imperialism

The various neoliberalisms may therefore be understood, as Foucault remarked in his lectures on modern governmentality, as programs for a particular technology of government which, rather than interfering directly with the individual, produces milieus in which older regimes of subjection and discipline have been made obsolete. Whereas disciplinary power once set up microcourts everywhere, now micromarkets are dispersed throughout the social field.[21] Economic governance aims at a kind of efficient and continuous self-employment in which competition, in all its manifestations, clears and penetrates the thicket of social relations. Commercial and competitive transactions, once punctually and locally organized, are now placed on a permanent footing. They carry with them the expectation that the complex web of interpersonal relationships can be coordinated through the multiplication of new explicit and implicit markets and their associated incentive structures. This also means that economic subjects no longer act simply as trading, producing, or consuming agents but function instead as fully fledged businesses, complete with corresponding motivational situations, action radii, and structural complexes. Households are redefined as miniature factories, individuals as microenterprises. If Foucault could speak in this regard of the formative, formalizing, and informing power of an enterprise culture for society, this does not mean that all forms of human behavior are now to be geared towards commercial and competitive imperatives. On the contrary, it means that the trace elements of market conformability in the totality of individual practices and movements, projects, goals, and decisions are to be activated. We are faced with the economization of everyday life and the "multiplication of the enterprise form within the social body."[22]

What, in this context, has very self-consciously been termed "economic imperialism"[23] gains in explanatory force with the waning of functional differentiation. Since the 1960s, it has centered on the new resource of "human capital." If this is taken to mean the totality of knowledge, skills, and qualifications which "assume the dual function of durable produced goods and consumer goods,"[24] then two essential dimensions are thereby disclosed. Besides detecting a push into non-economic terrain and an expansion of economic analysis to encompass hitherto neglected factors, we can see, on the one hand, that the binary opposition of capital and labor has been undermined and homogenized in a universal concept of capacity. From this viewpoint, the education, formation, and deployment of "labor-power" appear as an ongoing investment process, as one of the embodiments of capital as such, and hence as a source of future financial and emotional dividends. Relations between self and world have become investment concerns, while salaried employees have become "intrapreneurs" or "labor-power entrepreneurs." The "commercialization of everyday life" is further bound up with a new management style that specializes in the liquidation of older symbolic borders. Organizational structures become fluid, labor relations are remodeled in the image of an "anytime/any-place" economy, and individuals in active employment resemble labor nomads, wandering in a twilight zone between home and office, career and private life, personal and professional relationships.[25] The relevant catchphrases provide an overview of how reality is being programmed (that is to say, realized): Lifelong Learning, Flexibility, the Mobile Workforce, the Primacy of the Short Term—all these labels call for the dissolution of stable identities and reserve the future for a nebulous, shape-shifting self. Short-term contracts replace permanent institutions in professional and domestic, cultural and social domains. Those seeking expert advice on how to succeed in the job market will be informed about the demise of formalized work routines and the end of predictable careers and pathways through life. Having once been instructed to grasp their journey through life as a process of self-becoming, they are now urged to cultivate the art of becoming other.[26] Whereas the compulsion to identity once prevailed, now embracing the nonidentical has become the order of the day.

The saga of finance

On the other hand, investment goods and market relations are inevitably multiplied as a result. Genetic inheritance, education, training, knowledge, health, and family planning are all equally subject to the "economic approach," and economic analysis, as the science of human behavior and decision making in general, now refers to the totality of a social field whose dynamics and microstructures may be inferred according to the criteria of scarcity, necessity of choice, and opportunity costs. Here, according to Gary S. Becker and others, "shadow prices" can be calculated for the health and higher education systems, for schooling, science, and social relations; these are said to function analogously to the incentives provided by market prices.[27] It is hardly surprising, in the end, how a reminiscence of Aristotle returns here under a new guise, albeit one that would see the philosopher turning in his grave. If Malthus's theory of human population had already rested on the reciprocal relations between economic growth and fertility, these relations are now given a new, systematic form that conceives itself less as biopolitical than as bioeconomical. We are dealing with the vital standards of populations and hence, once again, with the procreative force of families, households, and domestic units. Marriage markets and divorce trends, the domestic and sexual division of labor, breeding habits, altruistic or selfish tendencies, relationships between the quality and quantity of children, birth and mortality rates, generational sequences and reproductive cycles, family planning and family politics: all these factors are to be evaluated and priced according to their marginal utility, that is, with a view to optimizing the relations between investment costs and foreseeable returns.

With that, not only does one of the primal scenes for the production of human capital come into view. More generally, the stakes of "filiative" capital—the entanglement of fecundity, procreation, and market activity, the linking of biological, social, and economic reproduction, the coupling of fertility and capital return—are realized here. The rationale provided for chrematistics is couched in terms suggesting a somnambulistic reprise of the Aristotelian question. Thus Gary Becker contends that his model of human capital as it pertains to the family "appears to be the first that relates fertility to interest rates." The reproduction of capital has finally attained "filiative" or dynastic predominance. That we are dealing here with a twentieth-century success story is unexpectedly claimed and illustrated with a narrative model for the synonymy of fertility and finance. The economist and Nobel laureate Becker programmatically cites the novelist and fellow Nobel laureate John Galsworthy, who has the narrator of his *Forsyte Saga* comment on the topic of "reproduction" in the following terms: "A student of statistics must have noticed that the birth rate had varied in accordance with the rate of interest for your money. Grandfather 'Superior Dosset' Forsyte in the early nineteenth century had been getting ten per cent for his, hence ten children. Those ten, leaving out the four who had not married, and Juley, whose husband Septimus Small had, of course, died almost at once, had averaged from four to five per cent for theirs, and produced accordingly."[28]

Such turns of phrase, in which the untrammeled forces of the market or of capital are directly tied back to social filiations, raise the prospect of an end to chrematistic theory, the effective consummation of chrematistics. The Aristotelian or Scholastic dichotomy of natural and artificial growth has been superseded. The very outsourcing of market and competitive dynamics and the decontextualization of capital flows were what made it possible for the social and political bond to be newly coded. That leaves its mark on the programs advanced by today's neo-Scholasticism, which unlike the Scholasticism of old is not concerned with preserving premodern, long-established economic modes but rather with bedding down the social field in the manner prescribed by postmodern economics. The resources of human capital represent the counterpart to the reorganization of the financial system since the 1970s. A process extending from the multiplication of market relations to the generalization of enterprise culture, from the formation of human capital to the economization of all relationship forms, exhausts itself in the "financialization" of the social field, in a kind of new covenant that unites social and economic reproduction even as it coordinates the life of the social body with the movement of capital.

Fault Zone

Field of desperation

All the same, it is hard to believe that neoliberal ideas could have been effectively and systematically woven into the fabric of society. We should remember that societies all but continuously generate attrition and loss, exclusion and dysfunction; they always contain potholes, tracts of wasteland, stagnant ponds of unproductiveness. Society is something "that leaks, financially, ideologically—there are leaks everywhere." Even Hegelian-Marxist orthodoxy would have to concede that social formations cannot be defined by way of "contradiction" and "division," nor do they necessarily offer themselves as arenas for the labor of the negative. Nothing—least of all capitalism itself—has ever run aground on its contradictions; on the contrary, the whole undertaking seems to function all the better "the more it breaks down."[1] Likewise, the latest proposals for the efficient, global reconciliation of society with the market amount to a series of directives which can only, at best, impose themselves regionally, provisionally, and in exceptional cases. Economic history itself calls for a more subtle capacity for differentiation and therefore turns out to be a field of desperation for economic theory. Just as the emergence of modern competitive societies cannot be understood as resulting from the continuous expansion, evolution, and monetization of local economic modes, so the success of capitalist agents cannot be explained by any putative respect for market rules on their part. Over a very long period of time, as Fernand

Braudel has shown, "age-old economic forms" and exchange relations of the most diverse kind continued to exist beneath the surface of the monetary economy, and skilled entrepreneurs have always operated in the realm of the "unaccustomed" and extraordinary, benefiting from patronage relations and privileged access to information, circumventing the laws of the market economy "in the most natural way" (in part with state support), and by no means considering themselves duty-bound to uphold liberal attitudes.[2]

It therefore seems appropriate to adopt a skeptical attitude towards all homogeneous economic models with systematic pretensions. A glimpse into the tangled mass of nonlinear historical developments invites us to block the process by which economic activity is subsumed under coherent economic logics. Primitive forms of allocation are not the same as markets, local markets are not the same as global markets, and these in turn are distinct from capitalist exchange relations. And even the brave new world of global finance has been beset by doubts as to how—if at all—its transactions still conform to classical market processes. Skepticism is all the more justified in view of a question raised by the vigorous adaptation of societies to the dynamics of capital turnover: how great a degree of dependence, from which laws, and with what consequences does this ongoing process suggest and indeed compel?

Keeping this question in mind will allow us to glimpse more than just a miscellany of isolated facts or historical corrections. What is at stake is the demand for consistency implicit in economic and financial theory. The very form of economic knowledge as a science stands in doubt, given that such a science will be without epistemic purchase unless, by definition, it fulfills the condition of a sufficiently constituted object—unless, that is, it can demonstrate some sort of really existing, systematic consistency. Economics legitimates itself as a science by demonstrating that the interplay of diverse factors and endeavors is capable of bringing forth a qualitatively different figure of order; and the possibility of economic theory stands or falls with the contention that economic dynamics are themselves lawfully regulated process forms.[3]

Confused empiricism

It is hardly surprising, then, that demonstrations of inadequate law-fulness and deficient systemic consistency are seen as attacks, not just on the status of political-economic orthodoxy but also on the scientific and theoretical claims made on behalf of the discipline of economics. A case in point is the episodic encounter from the 1960s that brought the Polish-French mathematician Benoit Mandelbrot into contact with American economic science and saw him carry out a series of investigations into the dynamics of price movements. Drawing on the examples of income distribution and long-term changes in cotton and security prices, Mandelbrot outlined an activity that resembles less a steadily flowing stream than sudden bouts of turbulence: an anomalous, wildly fluctuating perturbation which, in its unpredictable or monstrous outbursts, seemed determined by freak events rather than by rationally explicable processes.

In essence, there were four key findings that Mandelbrot, having first sifted through the data at IBM's Thomas J. Watson Research Center, proceeded to set out in numerous articles.[4] First, price changes cannot be traced along continuous pathways and infinitesimal variants; they are interrupted instead by nonlinear deviations and erratic variations. Discontinuous processes and abrupt leaps tend to prevail. Second, Mandelbrot noticed that over time small changes tend to be followed by small changes and large changes tend to be followed by large changes, such that gyrations and oscillations maintain or reinforce each other. This means that, third, even when examined over a longer time frame, successive price events do not hover around an average value. More precisely, they do not—unlike, say, the flurry of particles in Brownian motion—correspond to the probability of a normal distribution graphed on a Gauss or bell curve. They correspond instead to a hyperbolic or Pareto distribution in which a few large deviations determine the effect of the entire distributional structure, resulting in heavily skewed outliers, or so-called fat tails. Empirical distributions of price changes, Mandelbrot writes, "are too 'peaked' to be relative to samples of Gaussian populations." In addition, Mandelbrot observed that the geometric form of price changes remains constant regardless of the timescale applied: these changes are scale-invariant and have a self-similar or "fractal" structure. That is why, fourth, it is to be expected that over economic time sequences no predictable periodic cycles will emerge from the data but, at the most, fluctuations with "nonsense moments" and "nonsense periodicities." The regular ebbs and flows characteristic of "Joseph effects"—seven fat years here, seven lean years there—appear in combination with "Noah effects": deluge-like catastrophes, swings, and crashes.[5]

This account of market processes was bound to be provocative. According to Mandelbrot, background noise and trend amplifications, far from numbering among the incidental characteristics of price movements, reflect their "deeper truth," which can be described but not satisfactorily explained. In normal or Gaussian distributions, significant and extraordinary deviations can be ascribed to external causative factors; in the distributional patterns analyzed by Mandelbrot, the distinction between causal and accidental factors becomes blurred. The opposition between regular systemic functioning and exceptional occurrences now seems tenuous or irrelevant; and to the extent that the nonlinear dynamics of the market are here seen as being governed by indeterminate variables, processes are discerned which prove incompatible with notions of equilibrium. These processes break with certain "physicalisms" or "Newtonisms" favored by economic theory. Mandelbrot's debt to physics is evident, on the contrary, in his depiction of market activity as irreducibly stochastic, manifesting itself in irregular or "turbulent" event forms. The concept of turbulence—from the Latin *turba*, *turbo*, and *turbidus*—designates a murky continuum encompassing aspects of confusion, restlessness, immensity, and multiplicity; observing the phenomena which lie on this continuum means plunging into a dark and confused empiricism.

This is where Mandelbrot's economic investigations led him to traverse a field of objects also explored by the physical chemist Ilya Prigogine, who claimed to detect in it a fundamental repudiation of nineteenth-century physical and thermodynamic models. This field contains self-organizing structures that are far removed from states of equilibrium and which therefore tend to assume completely unpredictable behavioral forms, as exemplified in the spontaneous flow patterns of turbulent fluids. What is remarkable about such behavior is that it is by no means *simply* chaotic; it appears instead as a *structured* chaos in which a transition from an orderly "laminar" flow to an unsteady and "turbulent" flow takes place, resulting in continuous changes in speed and direction. Although, seen from a macroscopic point of view, states of turbulence appear to be utterly chaotic and irregular, on the microscopic level they prove to be highly organized. In effect, we are confronted here with states in which a system "wavers" on the threshold of different, equally viable directions of development, creating scope for a range of uncommon probabilities: at any given time, it remains uncertain which systemic state will come next. Prigogine refers in this context to the concept of *clinamen* in the physics of Epicurus or Lucretius: the tiny, unpredictable swerve that causes a particle to veer away from its trajectory, a chance deflection that generates the atomic swirl from which an entire universe may arise.[6]

The field of history

Against this background, Prigogine proclaimed a "science of becoming" whose phenomena would pertain more to the fields of society and history than to those of classical physics. Mandelbrot spells out the consequences for the figures of order underlying economic processes. What immediately becomes apparent is a collapse in predictability and statistically justified forecasts. Their place is taken by regular incalculability or incalculable order. Price movements resemble a fractally structured, organized chaos. Even when these movement profiles display certain regularities, they remain without prognostic value. In their fundamental irregularity, they frustrate the market-theoretical hope for pattern predictions or "catallactics." Recurring structural patterns can, at most, be put down to hindsight bias and "perceptual illusion": "Everything changes, nothing is constant."[7]

At the same time, the indeterminism that goes hand in hand with such unpredictability—a second-order indeterminism in which statistically probable dynamics, no longer covered by extreme value theorems, take on an almost meteorological character—opens up a paradoxical view of what is happening at any given time. Just as, in turbulent systems, a microscopic figure of order corresponds to macroscopic chaos, so deterministic variables on the microeconomic level—the rational conduct of market players, for example—can lead to movements with merely chance variables, and hence to irrational effects on the macroeconomic level.[8]

Markets tend to be influenced by fluctuating clusters of volatility; they are efficient *and* crazy at the same time. If they therefore appear to be limit figures of knowledge, then this is not least because, in markets, information is no longer distributed and communicated efficiently, that is, economically. To be sure, the organized chaos of turbulent motion is still, in principle, susceptible of representation; but the quantity of data needed to represent it verges on the incalculable:

The ideal case scenario that we could know and comprehend the movement of each individual particle in [turbulent] motion quickly proves illusory. In order to understand . . . a flow at a depth of one meter, for example, we would need to calculate the local speed in all three spatial dimensions in 10^{10} places. That equates to 10,000,000,000 or 10 billion places, and this would only capture the flow at a single point in time. Even though modern computers might be capable of storing so much data, it is doubtful whether such an exercise would provide us with any worthwhile knowledge.[9]

Acquiring information about such systems costs an exponential sum of information. From an economic point of view, this means that if efficient markets are defined by the efficient distribution of market information, then the market movements analyzed by Mandelbrot document an overtaxing or a breakdown of informational efficiency.

Leaving aside Mandelbrot's bemusement at economic theory's predilection for the models of nineteenth-century statistical physics, his own investigations raised profound doubts about the scientific status of their object. For if science is only possible when given patterns have a prospect of repeating themselves over time, thereby allowing for the extrapolation of laws, then the distributional patterns identified by Mandelbrot appear neither "conservative" nor "robust" enough to fulfill the concept of scientificity. And one must also, as Mandelbrot himself pointed out, be aware that "one faces a burden of proof that is closer to that of history . . . than that of physics."[10] In any event, the hypothesis of nonhomogeneous systems with abnormal distributions is "unscientific" in the sense that it operates with norm-free models; it has abandoned the search for universally valid rules and renounced all deterministic aspirations. A modified scientific format is in play here. The reliability of fixed laws makes way for a space of manifold bifurcations and potential rules. The pathways and variables of the economic universe have multiplied, and Mandelbrot's very mathematization of economic movements leads not into the promised land of systemic consistency but into a wilderness of historical contingency. What is called for is an idiosyncratic theory design that affirms the very inexplicability of its object. Markets resemble troubled waters whose complex behavior no invisible hand can smooth and no Ockham's razor can cut down to size. The simplest explanation is by no means the most correct. By claiming the intrinsic nonhomogeneity of economic processes and by systematically frustrating ideas of equilibrium, Mandelbrot's investigations represent a form of nomadic knowledge that has turned its back on the foundations and traditions of (neo)classical economics.

A theoretical approach of this kind, characterized as it is by a loss of intellectual certainty, potentially spells an end to economic theory; Mandelbrot may have been justified in once calling himself a "devil's advocate." This view came to be shared by political-economic orthodoxy itself. For the experts in the field, Mandelbrot's market scenarios appeared far from promising; one even denounced them as a "mishmash of pure nonsense and tricks." What many found particularly objectionable was the retraction of the economic object, amounting to a ruinous negation of self-regulating market mechanisms and economic systematicity: "It's not that easy to deal with those predictions in a systematic way." In the end, if Mandelbrot was right, "almost all our statistical tools [would be] obsolete. . . . Surely, before consigning centuries of economic work to the ash pile, we should like to have some assurance that all our work is truly useless." For "Mandelbrot, like Prime Minister Winston Churchill before him, promises us not utopia, but blood, sweat, toil and tears."[11] In the 1970s Mandelbrot temporarily withdrew from the field of economics; his attack on economic theory's ideas of system, its figures of equilibrium and order, remained episodic.

Even if the resonance of Mandelbrot's disconcerting models proved short-lived and resulted at best in scattered attempts to adapt them to the seriousness of oikodicy (things always become more serious, Deleuze and Guattari once remarked, when nondeterministic forms of knowledge have to be brought into line with "determinism"[12]), the questions they posed concerning the mechanisms governing financial markets opened up a polemogenic field. Under the aegis of various neoliberalisms, financial systems had been set up to run theoretically, practically, and technically on the model provided by efficient, perfectly functioning markets. Financial activity appeared as pars pro toto of the economy as a whole. Increasingly, however, concerns have been voiced that what articulates itself in the logic of financial transactions is not so much a consummation of spontaneous market processes as their distortion and unraveling. For some time now, a motley crew of devil's advocates has been insisting that the turbidity and tumultuousness of financial markets cannot simply be pacified through the judicious application of rebalancing mechanisms or through the stabilizing interplay of rational participants and systemic rationality.

The intermittent financial crises of recent decades have thus lent weight to the quite understandable surmise that the capitalist economy is by no means behaving as it ought to behave. According to the probability theorems of efficient markets, the recurring crashes since 1987 had a risk factor of one in tens of billions and thus should never have occurred. They therefore confirm the hypotheses that financial markets may not be real markets after all and that their price-setting mechanisms are not necessarily market-compliant.[13] For all their evident undesirability, these so-called crises indicate that exceptional cases may well play an integral part in the regular functioning of the system. At the same time, they attest to a crisis in the theoretical model that places its trust in the inherent self-stabilizing tendencies of financial markets. And insofar as crises, irregularities, and turbulences signify nothing less than that the present status of a system does not necessarily derive from its past status, or its future status from its present one, they feed doubts as to whether classical and neoclassical concepts—concepts such as equilibrium, self-regulation, efficiency, rational expectations, the coordinating force of price signals, and so on—are sufficient to grasp the dynamics of financial processes. The question is thus whether the specific character of economic processes manifests itself in notionally "timeless" phases of stability or, on the contrary, in states of exception, in the destabilizing irruption of historical time.

With that, a distinction is introduced that is as much quantitative as it is qualitative. On the one hand, there is copious evidence to show how the peculiar materiality of the finance economy has become divorced from the materiality of production, how its turnover has exceeded by multiples the volume of trade in commodities and become "weightless." Whereas productive capacity has barely risen since the midtwentieth century relative to freight and tonnage, value creation has tripled over the same period.[14] On the other hand, we may inquire to what extent the fluctuations of the finance economy are still modeled on elementary exchange processes and the mechanisms of goods turnover. According to the various divisions of the classical schools, monetary exchange functions as a kind of veil that merely covers real economic relations without affecting them in any specific way. Milton Friedman could still maintain that "despite the importance of enterprises and money in our actual economy . . . , the central characteristic of the market technique of achieving coordination is fully displayed in the simple exchange economy," that is, an economy "that contains neither enterprises nor money."[15] In the meantime, however, attention has been drawn to the autonomous logic of monetary circulation and to the specificity of associated decision-making processes, dynamics, and relations of dependence. Capitalism simply cannot be understood in isolation from capitalists and capitalist practices.

Liquidity

Financial transactions do more than just intermittently ascertain appropriate prices and correct valuations. Since they are realized or consummated in payment promises that become loans or investments and since these are realized in financial markets, which in turn fulfill themselves in the trading of stocks and shares, their main purpose is clearly to procure liquidity. In mobilizing capital, such transactions respond to both the needs of borrowers and the claims of lenders, and they serve to make investments—along with advance payments in the form of credit—possible in the first place. That is why payable prices are never self-present and self-oblivious, so to speak; they are never structured like momentarily passing points in time. Rather, they emerge as a kind of advance memory. Directly inspired by risk outlooks and forecast rates of return, they are determined by payments that do not occur now but will take place in the future. These are prices, then, that constitute themselves via expectations of future prices. Profit has to be imagined before it can be reaped.

Put differently, monetary and credit transactions, investments and capital markets present themselves as time-critical, "time-consuming" processes. They rest on future forecasts and "profit expectations, so that the decisions to invest are always made under conditions of uncertainty. Because of uncertainty, investors and their financiers seek asset and liability structures that provide protection against unfavorable contingencies and adjust their portfolios as history unfolds and their views about the likely development of the economy change."[16] The mere allocation of quantities of goods makes way for deliberations on earnings forecasts and risk outlooks. As a result, current price horizons are linked up on a feedback loop with future price horizons. On this terrain, markets can no longer gravitate around existing supplies, scarce resources, and fixed or "real" value references. Participants do not operate with known quantities; instead, they attempt to evaluate a contingent future based on how it is currently valued by the market itself. With that, apparently reliable factors like supply and demand—and their stabilizing force—become not just unknown but unknowable. Supply and demand mechanisms only hold sway in a realm where one operates with fixed budgets, not one where financing terms and future expectations are at stake. Accordingly, any demonstration that the exchange economy could be coherent, retributive, distributive, and allocative would have nothing to say about how the finance economy actually works. Financial markets never reach saturation point, and demand for capital goods is to be kept strictly separate from demand for consumer goods.

With that, we have arrived at a perspective adopted by several proponents of a radicalized Keynesianism. They show little interest in advocating an active monetary politics, a politics of welfare-state interventions in times of crisis. Keynesian positions do not simply compete with market-liberal ideas against a background of common consent on the status of their object. Rather, their principal aim is to reestablish the field of finance economics in strict delimitation from market-economic conceptions—a maverick approach that has assured them, from the 1970s until recently, a more or less apocryphal relevance within the canon of political-economic doctrines. Analogously to Mandelbrot's antideterministic models, nothing less is at stake here than the constitution of an alternative knowledge of the capitalist process. Under the condition of an elementary financing process—under the condition, that is, that the financial market deals with questions of liquidity and structures itself via investment and credit liabilities—money cannot be understood as a neutral or at most veiling medium of exchange in economic transactions. Rather, it presents itself as a medium with its own efficacy and power. So-called real economic measures depend directly on their mediation through monetary and financial measures. Price formation is understood neither as a way to determine the relative weighting to be accorded to scarce resources, nor—as in quantity theories of money—as a function of the adjustable amount of money on the market. And the logic of choice is not characterized by conditions of scarcity but by the condition of uncertainty. Above all, financial processes by no means function according to the model of a self-correcting, self-optimizing system. Instead, the very systematicity of the system is called into question. Whereas the various equilibrium theories could offer, at best, only anecdotal explanations for financial crises, here these "devastating logical holes" become the presupposition for a different epistemic and theoretical model, a different configuration of the object of finance economics. They form the basis of an attempt to understand anomalous processes and systemic instability as resulting from the normal functioning of the capitalist economy.[17] The modern financial system, along with its institutions and cash flows, should thus be contemplated from the vantage point of the end of oikodicy and situated in a realm subject to the impact of contingent events, historical ages, and periods.

Doxa

This requires that we accept the fact that the financial market as an institution serves to procure liquidity, and that it can only do so through speculation. The latter, for its part, operates in specular fashion. The earliest accounts of stock market trading already noted that the real facts consist in expectations of facts, a trend that can be described in general terms as a self-reflexive tendency built into financial activity.[18] To the extent that the purchase of financial assets takes place as a purchase of expected returns, payable prices are set in anticipation of foreseeable prices. The course of events is determined not by what was or what is, but by what could, might, or probably will be. The financial market functions as a system of anticipations which stakes economic behavior on second-guessing what the market itself thinks the future may bring. Current expectations thus do not simply anticipate future events; rather, future events are coconstituted by expectations of future events and consequently acquire virulence in the present. The present is produced by "beforehand" effects, as *hýsteron próteron* of its own future. With that, we find ourselves caught up in a game of exponentially raised expectations in which players observe each other's observations and anticipate each other's possible anticipations.

This specular or reflexive structure means, first of all, that information circulating on the market is justifiable only in doxological, not epistemological terms. Valid knowledge of the "real," "true," or "fundamental" value of things is not to be had. Instead, valuations emerge from opinions mirroring opinions about opinions. Financial markets function as an ongoing balancing act in an environment where the pressure to conform is all-pervasive. Resonances of collective views, congealed into norms, circulate in the form of prices; and to the extent that an opinion is articulated with each payment about what general expectation generally expects to occur, decision-making and judgment profiles are increasingly conventionalized. That is not to rule out speculations against the market or isolated actions on the part of skeptics or "contrarians." In this respect, it is even possible to detect an affinity with the relationship between opinion and fashion, given that the establishment of fashion trends likewise requires a faintly paradoxical attitude of clinging to the transient and conforming to the extravagant.

Expressed in Kantian terms, the form taken by this economic judgment therefore has little in common with cognitive judgments. If anything, it displays an aesthetic character, since judgments of taste (according to Kant) stake a claim to "general validity" by invoking an "indeterminate norm" that—itself conceptually indeterminate—could "demand universal assent."[19] It is not by chance that Keynes chose to illustrate the choreography of financial markets with the notorious image of a beauty contest. According to this image, prices, like the "prettiest faces," are set by "the competitor whose choice most nearly corresponds to the average preferences of the competitors as a whole; so that each competitor has to pick, not those faces which he himself finds prettiest, but those which he thinks likeliest to catch the fancy of the other competitors, all of whom are looking at the problem from the same point of view."[20] Current market opinion is based on "what average opinion expects average opinion to be," and judgments are made on the assumption that a majority of judgment acts will coincide in them. Smith's invisible hand has made way for an open push for conventionality. To the extent that financial markets operate as systems to cover financing costs, they may be understood as mechanisms for the autopoietic production of *doxa*, in which rational expectations and preferences are only truly rational if they directly coincide with common opinion and find consensus in normative ideas. Financial truths are built on conventions, conventionalism dictates the episteme of markets, and every theoretical justification only ratifies this doxological substrate. Precisely as the subject of all that can be known, the market renders the distinction between knowledge and opinion obsolete. From a governance point of view, those who call for a deregulation of financial markets are demanding nothing less than a symbiosis of economic and intellectual conformities, a machine to produce normalizing trends. That also explains how economic processes can be quantified; as Gabriel Tarde observed long ago, they are regulated by the "accord of collective judgments," by the conformist attitudes and beliefs of the many.[21]

Feedback

Prices on financial markets are thus not set by the same mechanisms as those which govern commodity markets. Price levels do not establish themselves and regulate the market according to the model of scarce volumes and given quantities. Far from representing rock-solid "fundamentals," they circulate through the market as highly potent spectral values. Precisely for that reason, however, trend amplifications and positive feedback are not catastrophic exceptions to the status quo but functional elements endogenous to the system. Rising prices reflect public appraisals of worth and prompt upward revaluations, whereas falling prices make the swift anticipation of further devaluations appear entirely rational. The balancing interplay of supply and demand is inverted, giving rise to the paradoxical impression that cheap financial assets are expensive and expensive financial assets are cheap and offer good value for money. Higher prices increase demand rather than lowering it.

The Princeton economist Huyn Shong Shin detected an analogy between interdependencies of this kind and the effects of the feedback problems that plagued London's "Millennium Bridge"—a footbridge spanning the Thames between Tate Modern and Saint Paul's Cathedral—upon its opening in 2000. The bridge's slight horizontal shaking at 1 hertz caused the hundreds of pedestrians streaming across it to involuntarily adjust their steps. Whereas a mass of uncoordinated individual movements would ordinarily prove too diverse for a single combined movement to emerge (even soldiers break step when crossing a bridge), in this case the structure's tiny, haphazard oscillations caused civilian feet to adapt both to the sway and to each other's adaptations. Varying gaits were imperceptibly synchronized into lock-step motion, thereby generating and amplifying a sideways movement. And the very randomness of all these different walking styles gave rise to self-amplifying patterns, to what the engineers called "synchronous lateral excitation": "the critical threshold for the number of pedestrians that started the wobble was 156," beyond which "the wobble increased at a sharply higher rate." The elegant structure had to be closed to the public and retrofitted with fluid dampers. In a similar way, the economist concludes, price fluctuations on financial markets lead to rational adaptive reactions, which produce coherent figures of order, which in turn result via positive feedback in a "perfect storm." Like the wobbly bridge, "financial markets are the supreme example of an environment where individuals react to what's happening around them, and where individuals' actions affect the outcomes themselves." Or, "The pedestrians on the Millennium Bridge are rather like modern banks that react to price changes, and the movements in the bridge itself are rather like price changes in the market. So, under the right conditions, price changes will elicit reactions from the banks, which move prices, which elicit further reactions, and so on."[22]

We are not just concerned here with identifying the self-amplifying tendencies and "trend-chasing" of short-term speculations, nor is it solely a matter of hoping that on financial markets—unlike on sandy racetracks—horses can be spurred to victory by having bets placed on them. Rather, dynamics of this kind quite fundamentally shape the way long-term processes, too, can unfold without ever coming to rest in states of equilibrium, attesting to a dynamic imbalance and an irreducible

instability in the functioning of the system. Thus the Keynesian economist Hyman Minsky, until recently something of an unheard voice in
the ensemble of political economy, demonstrated from the 1960s onward
how stability phases lead to increased volatility, balancing efforts precipitate disruptions, and beautiful upswings result in manifest imbalances in
financial activity. Accordingly, under the conditions of a modern finance
economy—characterized by profit-oriented market players, an investment
banking system, and trade with fixed and financial assets—it is precisely
the most stable and promising economic conditions which set off a diabolical financing cycle. Here too a genuinely capitalist structure is in effect.
The elementary units of this economy consist not in exchange relations
but in liability structures. Investment decisions and financing decisions are
interlinked and tied to an uncertain future and its yield risks. The starting point is thus the temporal rejection of a money-now-for-money-later
correlation. Current profits validate past decisions, and present investment
and financing decisions are determined by expectations of future profit.

Given these premises, there seems to be no good reason why, in
periods of robust growth with positive long-term outlooks, the scope of
investments should not be expanded beyond the limits of secured finance.
It makes perfectly good sense to keep investing and to intensify financing
demands against the justified hope of future capital returns. That leads,
on the one hand, to investment income being reinvested rather than used
to repay loans. Placing their trust in a "speculative" capitalization process,
investors take out new loans to refinance existing loans as they fall due.
On the other hand, the growing hunger for finance on the part of profit-
oriented financial institutions motivates the invention of novel currencies
and financial instruments in the form of money substitutes or portfolios.

Theory of instability

In this process, in which every financial innovation and every broad-
ened use of earlier financing practices increases the volume of available
finance, we enter into a situation where—put simply—a positive feedback
loop links soaring investment, higher profits, rising prices for financial assets
(such as stocks and shares), and higher investment costs. Put differently,
favorable economic conditions make it easier to raise capital, and investment

volumes increase accordingly. The amount of money effectively in circulation grows, and the concurrently rising cost of returns on investment increases both demand for loans and the willingness of lenders to finance them. In this investor-friendly climate, security margins are scaled back, liquidity preference declines, money supply is increased, and ever more debt piles up. The expansion of financial activity triggers an escalation in asset values and prices for investment goods. According to Minsky, this necessarily results in a pyramid structure in which outstanding debts are offset by further and riskier investments. The fall in liquid assets relative to the market value of capital assets held in portfolios is matched by a surge in liabilities that can only be offset by rising net profits, a recursive increase in external financing and debt servicing. This gives rise to a self-perpetuating and self-accelerating system that works itself, through positive feedback to its own horizon of expectations, into a state of speculative "euphoria."[23]

Liability structures and a general context of indebtedness—Walter Benjamin's debt- and guilt-ridden cult of capitalism—thus feed directly back to inner-worldly expectations, and the critical factor of this dynamic lies in the relationship between two countervailing capital flows, in the relationship, that is, between investment income and debt obligations, fixed or long-term liabilities, and foreseeable yet always uncertain and variable profit outlooks. Eventually, a precarious situation arises where compliance with existing financing contracts requires either new loans or asset sales. This can result in exorbitant financing options and rising investment costs, on the one hand, and in losses and pricing pressure on secondary markets and hence falling capital costs, on the other. When an increase in liquidity preference ensues, thereby posing a threat to liquidity as such, or when, conversely, a decline in the price of financial assets takes place, the flow-on effects can spread from individual participants back to the entire economic system via the cascade-like interdependences guaranteed by the banking structure. The result is a spiral of declining capital expenditure, falling profits, and decreasing investment. The functioning of the system has reached its peripeteia; proceedings become completely uncertain and assume a turbulent character. A continuation of operations and a collapse now appear equally likely.

Minsky's thesis of financial instability accordingly suggests that manifest crises and breakdowns are not simply caused by external tremors, by fiscal or political coups de théâtre; rather, they are brought about by the parameters and endogenous movements of the financial economy itself. Unlike cybernetic and self-regulating systems, the financial market is inclined to be spooked by its own tranquillity and destabilized by its own stability. The very efficiency of its functioning turns out to be utterly dysfunctional. Every period of peace and quiet is transitory, and in a world with capitalist finance, as Minsky remarks, "it is simply not true that the pursuit by each unit of its own self-interest will lead an economy to equilibrium." An analysis of supply and demand—with the prospect of self-adjustment and equilibrium—does not explain the workings of a capitalist economy, and its financial processes operate in such a way that they themselves generate "endogenous destabilizing forces." This means that the financial institutions of capitalism are "inherently disruptive. Thus, while admiring the properties of free markets, we must accept that the domain of effective and desirable free markets is restricted."[24]

2007–

So far as capital markets are concerned, then, crises are always crises of circulation and hence of liquidity. Perhaps we find them so disturbing because they shake to its very foundations the theoretical and practical faith we ordinarily place in the workings of a self-regulating market. The reciprocal relationship between financial innovation, investment volume, and debt circulation can plausibly be described as the mainspring of the finance economy over the last four decades. Even the most recent "crisis," beginning in 2007, conforms to this familiar profile. Here too a liquidity paradox reemerged to devastating effect: liquidity dried up at precisely the moment when it was needed and wanted the most.[25] In this case, financial markets initially registered positive feedback from various capitalization processes which had been set off by benign economic conditions and driven by fully rational decision-making procedures and expectations. Rising real estate prices since the 1990s, especially in the United States, fueled the need for finance and led to the creation of new financial instruments. This in turn caused capital returns to increase, intensifying the search for further investment avenues and resulting in even higher property prices. Leaving aside the momentous changes in institutional settings that facilitated such developments (for example, the repeal of the Glass-Steagall Act in 1999, which regulated the separation of business and investment banking; the Basel II Accord, which accommodated equity requirements to market conditions; or the market-friendly influence of ratings agencies), two business practices, above all, were thought to have perfected or fully rationalized financial operations. Between them, these two practices proved capable of unleashing the euphoria or accelerating its spread.

On the one hand, the increased demand for finance was met by so-called securitization. Lenders (commercial or mortgage banks) con-solidated contracted property loans into bonds, offset them with interest repayments, split them into different tranches, and sold them on second-ary markets as asset-based securities. Investment banks combined these with other loans and repackaged them as collateral debt obligations, assets with varying prospects of risk and return. In this way, coursing down multiple channels and byways, not only could finance offers be increased at will, but existing liabilities—that is, credit risks—were also removed from the original lenders' balance sheets, dispersed, diversified, and to some extent insured, all through the logic of those derivatives in which the perspectives of sellers with an aversion to risk happily coincided with those of buyers with an affinity for it. The IMF's *Global Stability Report* from April 2006 could still speak in this respect of the "new participants, with differing risk management and investment objectives (including other banks seeking portfolio diversification), [who] help to mitigate and absorb shocks to the financial system, which in the past affected primarily a few systemically important financial intermediaries."[26] That meant, not least, that individual risk documentation was replaced by an aggregate overview of the statistical distribution of risk potentials. This was done through an accounting practice, "value at risk," that allowed singular risk events to be absorbed by being bundled over the weight of foreseeable normal distributions. Future probabilities were modeled on current ones. This strategy was supplemented, finally, by an ominous species of derivatives called "credit default swaps," a kind of loan default insurance which made it possible for especially profit-oriented, risk-tolerant investors to purchase risk items from lenders' balance sheets. Financing needs were covered by the sale of purchased risk as insolvency became a tradable commodity.

This amalgam of derivatives and credit money can be understood as a self-reflexive means for creating money and hence as the higher-order circulation of insolvency.[27]

On the other hand, consistent use was made of the "mark-to-market" procedure in balancing relevant values. In ascertaining the value of current assets and liabilities in the investment and credit cycle, reference was made to the prices at which the corresponding bonds and securities were trading on stock exchanges or in similar markets (or the prices at which they could be expected to trade). The value of things, after all, consists in nothing other than their price, and the valuation of a financial instrument can be legitimated by pointing to its current market cost. Here, once again, appeal could be made to the logic of efficient markets—to the idea, that is, that "if prices aggregate the information and beliefs of market participants, then this is the best estimate of value."[28] Accordingly, current market prices directly determine the worth of capital stock. Higher prices increase the book value of equity capital and assets, hence also making it easier for companies to tap into investment funds and to secure lines of credit. This efficient script completed the financial mechanism. What results is a textbook example of how markets are meant to operate. Price variations immediately induce reactions in balance sheets in the form of further price variations, while rising real estate prices directly flow on to rising capital values, higher investment returns, and decreased risk potential.[29] Measurable risk declines with rising asset prices, additional capital is made available for reinvestment, and a process is initiated which—as described by Minsky—leads from secured finance via financial speculation to pyramid financing schemes.

Yet when property prices stagnated in 2006 and then began to fall from the autumn of that year, doubts about the current and future value of capital assets, especially so-called subprime loans, became increasingly widespread. Price estimates plunged amidst growing concerns that values had become indeterminate or indeterminable; the mutually reinforcing tendency of progressive movements was checked; and the signals set by the market price system—together with their associated incentives—assumed an altogether erratic character. When the probability of loan defaults increased as the first homeowner bankruptcies were declared, new investments failed to materialize, credit lines were squeezed, ratings agencies started to downgrade securities, and interest rates on cash markets soared; the reverse adaptive movement set in, an adjustment to adjustments resulting in "synchronous lateral excitation." Economic rationality regressed along the path of financing chains. The market for real estate loans faltered and collapsed, assets of all kinds had to be sold off to meet refinancing demands, while capital markets came under pressure and allowed property prices to sink even further. And because capital markets, unlike stock exchanges, cannot be temporarily shut down, the self-perpetuating fall in prices for property, mortgages, and their derivatives left behind "liquidity black holes." Each of these movements intensified the oscillations in the system. Procyclical processes and resonance catastrophes are part of the system, and the most recent crash of the American mortgage market was therefore probably only the catalyst, not a sufficient reason for the subsequent worldwide collapse.

The resource of time

The general conclusion to be drawn from all this is that the advancement of market-compatible mechanisms—the incentive of price signals, the efficient interconnection of participants, the universalization of finance markets and bank-like structures—led to paralysis in the system and the cessation of its allocative functions. Rational operations and players produce irrational effects, and if there is an invisible hand at work here, then it can only be described as diabolical in nature. In essence, the market dreams the dream of its own endlessness and is troubled only by the secular circumstance that, owing to the limited, this-worldly means of finite participants, it finds itself confronted time and again by the barrier of insolvency. In the end, this means that here, under the conditions of modern finance, a mutual heightening of security and insecurity takes place similar to that attested by Dirk Baecker for the logic of the banking industry as a whole. Stabilization is attained through the spread and transfer of instabilities. It is not simply a matter of noting how oscillation phases with positive feedback necessarily lead to the short-term accumulation of internal risks. Rather, the very actuarial logic informing the latest financing strategies served at once to foster and to intensify, to produce and to disguise systemic risk. Just as banks tend to build risks into their forms of investment, to diversify them and sell them on, thereby making a profitable business out of the risks of solvency reproduction,[30] so too in the dynamics of the derivatives trade and in the "securitization food chain"—perfect embodiments of capitalist or financial rationality—risks are insured with more risks: they are outsourced, spread, and distributed along different temporal horizons. With that, a direct motive is given for raising the threshold for risk exposure. Furthermore, whenever price risks are hedged through the dispersal of price risks and speculative deals are hedged through speculative deals, thereby creating new risk markets to provide security against risk, this has the effect of offsetting current against future risks, which in turn are offset against the risks of future futures. Present markets are determined by an endless series of anticipations, and their fluctuations depend not merely on their multiple futures but on whatever occurs subsequent to those futures.

The vanishing point of the process thus lies in a future after the future. But that is precisely what suggests or indeed imposes a strict distinction between different perspectives, between (calculable) risks and (incalculable) uncertainties. On the one hand, the future—time as an infinite and inexhaustible resource—is presupposed in these operations and in the internal logic of the system. Risk can only be transferred effectively if every outstanding future can be extended into a further future and if this temporal expansion can be continued indefinitely. By the logic of efficient markets, the calculable version of risk flows can be maintained solely on the condition that current risks are modeled on the probability of past risks and the risks of future presents are modeled on the risk probability of present futures. Each future must be the statistical shadow of its past for reliable knowledge of the future to be established. Risk probability thus acquires an "ergodic" structure, one which dictates that all future event populations are dispersed analogously to current probabilities, in conformity to a relation in which a series of a thousand throws of a single die equates to a single throw of a thousand dice. Keynes had also described this as a case of cardinal probability in action, where the relationship between individual risky events can be captured in a ratio since they occur independently of each other and without correlation. This "real" risk is computed in a way similar to that which pertains in the realm of solidary groups and pension funds: for a fire insurance society, one house fire here or there does nothing to affect the probability that fires could break out elsewhere.[31] Under the condition of an indefinitely prolonged future, the comforting prospect of reinsurance via statistically established normal distributions persists in the risk pyramids of the derivatives trade. To the extent that future probabilities always correspond to current ones, it would appear that whatever is decided and acted on today will have no impact on the range of future possibilities.

On the other hand, however, this treatment of event populations as commensurable—defying the predictions of efficient-market theorists— proves invalid as soon as risky decisions are understood as time-critical operations which, moreover, enter into a feedback loop with other risky operations. One can only insure oneself against one's own risks by creating risks for others, who for their part must create further risks in order to insure themselves. All this presupposes that time frames are finite, that allotted terms expire, deadlines arrive, payments fall due, and future presents always differ from present futures. Economic time series are thus by no means stationary or isotropic. The circumstances surrounding economic decisions remain neither neutral nor homogeneous over time, and they call for continuous adaptive reactions. The more the future—from an actuarial point of view—is used to profile current decisions, the more the success of this strategy depends on the future actually conforming to expectations (or the expectable spread of possible outcomes). The future and its futures could then appear as an acceptable risk, but "the devil does not necessarily wish future presents to conform to the present future."[32] What happens is always different from what one thinks will happen. And this means that, as soon as a future present arrives, its difference from the future one had once counted on arriving and factored into one's deliberations is also actualized. The circular temporal structure of the finance industry is thus precisely what provokes unexpected futures to return to haunt the present. As Elena Esposito has remarked, that has been evident in all so-called crises, including the most recent. Accordingly, every risk appraisal is based on a current estimation of the future calculated by processing past data. This yielded the elements necessary for granting credit. The expected rise in property prices to cover the bankruptcy rate was already accounted for in the present. When prices sank instead, it had to be conceded "that one had erred not only in the decision but also in the constructed future, since the future now only imposes obligations instead of opening up possibilities. One must now continue paying for a project that no longer corresponds to reality, yet which cannot be changed or can be changed only by incurring additional costs."[33] The future as a realm of insured possibilities has now become costlier than expected, or it has simply ceased to exist.

Back from the future

Yet this means we have done more than just made chance mistakes and be deceived in our expectations; we have quite consequentially contributed to producing a future different from the probable or expected one: "One used a different future than that which one had ushered in." This is exactly what happened in the chain dynamics of securities underwriting securities. Insofar as current credits were guaranteed by bonds, which in turn were backed by future debtor payments and further derivatives, it was no longer clear, after the first bankruptcies were declared and expectations had to be adjusted accordingly, whether the circulating loans still represented the prospect of future profits or merely a faded and now untenable promise.[34]

At this point, available capital could no longer be distinguished from pure phantasm. Having banked on an endlessly distended future while at the same time using up its resources, we find that the present use of the future has exhausted the reserve of time currently at our disposal. Precisely because the present here depends on a future that is in turn oriented to the present, since the present manifests itself as the effect of a future that it has itself initiated, the power of the future thus accumulated expresses itself in paradoxical fashion. Financing chains ensure or insure the continuous procurement of liquidity, but as soon as an insured loss (i.e., a bankruptcy) appears here or there, the available future is depleted even as current liquidity is reduced; the range of possibilities shrinks in the present itself. Now one simply has less time or less future at one's disposal. The insurance or "securitization" of future event sequences returns as an incursion of uncontrollable contingency, and the technologies deployed to control, colonize, or defuturize the future end up transforming it into an unforeseen event impinging on the here and now.[35] A *revenant* of a most peculiar kind, the specter of capital always comes back from its own future.

Whereas, within this financing system and under the condition of an endless supply of time, the logic of securitization and the associated capitalist process thus place their trust in the continuous transformation of uncertainty into calculable probability, a glimpse at the system as a whole brings the opposite dynamic into view. Here future presents appear as unforeseeable precisely because they were produced by anticipation (and by anticipating anticipations) in the here and now. Dealing with risk has become a highly risky endeavor, and the financial architecture of the last few decades, this latest capitalist innovation push, has in all probability proved itself to be a "complete failure."[36] It nonetheless serves to illustrate, in a quite fundamental way, the logic behind the financial system and the capitalist market's mode of operation. When confronted by uncertain futures, economic rationality pursues a strategy of transforming decisions into mere risks, into the calculable and constructive internal operations of a self-referential system[37]; yet this approach to risk management has itself become a systemic risk, increasing the rate of unknown probabilities in the functional whole. It reveals a hypocritical performance in which the negation of risk entails its affirmation (and vice versa). The system's immanent operations have blurred the difference between risk and uncertainty and thereby made it all the more telling. Uncertainty—that is, potentiated future—is here not simply an object of expectation and foresight; rather, it intrudes into the current present to dictate its course. The lack of certainty is precisely what intervenes in the here and now. Under these conditions, we should face up to the fact that endogenous market processes function inefficiently, their cycles appearing both normal and traumatic in equal measure; economic theory itself admits to operating with vague prospects and offers at best a "science of imprecision." It should therefore by no means come as a surprise if clear-sighted stockbrokers and traders occasionally dabble in Stoic meditation exercises and recommend Seneca's *Moral Letters* to each other.[38]

That endows so-called crises with a peculiar event format. If crises can generally be understood as involving a confusion of experiential spaces and horizons of expectation or, in Blumenberg's words, a "capacity to experience times of disintegration,"[39] then the critical dynamic of the finance economy is structured by its rejection of distinct temporal orders. While financial markets strive for secular eternity, while their subjects dream of transcending their own mortality, and while capital itself is impelled to vanquish the obscure forces of time and eliminate the obstacles on its path to an unlimited future, this chrematistic striving is always haunted by measurable terms, fixed appointments, due payments—in short, by the conditions of finite historical periodicities. Economic time is measureless, empty, indeterminate, proleptic, and abstract; historical times are full, concrete, particular, irreversible, and limited. Just as the vicissitudes of historical time are incompatible with the regime of the economic temporal order, so the limitless time demands of capitalist processes impose themselves on the existence of finite things and beings, manifesting there as a kind of futuristic pressure. In DeLillo's words, "the future becomes urgent"; it weighs on the present and makes its presence felt by mortgaging lived and livable time periods. What is critical is thus not just the question of how the force of time codifies economic actions and event chains, but also the question of how it becomes entangled with temporal patterns of limited duration and finite occurrences.

[margin annotation: economic / historical time]

End of oikodicy

With that, a long-overdue end to oikodicy is also heralded. After years spent demanding that the unreliable behavior of individuals be brought to reason via market mechanisms, we now have to concede that financial markets (as the markets of all markets) operate in such a way that their rational decision-making processes systematically produce the very opposite of rationality. The dual origin of the oikodicy in moral philosophy and cosmology not only motivated a scientific self-understanding on the part of political economy; it also promoted an image of markets as the essence or *ēidos* of social harmony. That resulted in a self-legitimating circle by which the market form was theoretically justified and theoretical knowledge about markets was normatively privileged. This free-floating, self-founding theoretical construct is held together solely by the presumption of self-regulating, self-optimizing, and smoothly functioning market dynamics, or by the claim that "the pure theory of economics is a science which resembles the physico-mathematical sciences in every respect."[40] To this day, it still inspires some of the hoary legends lurking at the heart of political-economic knowledge: that there are "pure" economic facts, that they form a consistent system, that this system functions efficiently, and that all this follows an evolutionary process which leads from situations of simple necessity, via marketplaces, trade networks, and the monetary economy, all the way up to a global financial "order." Such legends could be identified without difficulty as ideological were it not for the fact that political economy has actually created the very economic conditions it feels called on to analyze—from the ubiquitous hubbub of competition to the present-day financial system.

The persistence of these legends is all the more surprising given that even healthy human common sense—as embodied, say, by someone suited to a career in business—has begun to doubt that growth creates employment, that privatization leads to improved standards of care, that the market is based on fair competition, and that competition in general tends to the universal dispersal of affluence. From Marx or Max Weber onwards, the critique of political economy has been spurred on by the riddle of the rational irrationalities in the capitalist process, and the end of oikodicy consequently requires that economic knowledge be denaturalized, that it be released from its old, providential strictures and transferred to an open historical field. What is required, in other words, is that economics be divorced from economic theory. With that, economic operations no longer appear as a homogeneous system or order; rather, they emerge as a conglomerate of diverse cultural technologies with which people seek to master uncertainties, preempt dangers, structure communications, interpret their relations with the material world, gain the upper hand over their rivals, and improve their profit outlooks. Realism suggests that we direct our attention from the modeling of consistent system ideas to the heterogeneity of plural origins, contributing factors, and actual practices. After all, capitalism is neither the realization of social Providence nor the bearer of any grand historico-philosophical mission, and it is certainly not concerned with maintaining coherence and staying true to itself by any possible means. It is not about to collapse from exhaustion and die a natural death, but nor will it guarantee the spontaneous and universal allocation of wealth. It does not run and finance itself. To acknowledge that it is produced, supported, and maintained by social and political activities, however, is to pose the question of the objective and normative limits of its fields of operation. Markets cannot be shielded from crises and breakdowns, but our dependence on them can be reduced. Consumer goods and financial assets, the labor force, health, education, or natural resources cannot all be divvied up according to one and the same market logic, nor can they all be "capitalized" to the same extent by an all-(de)regulating market mechanism. The finance industry's recent and entirely understandable appeal to be rescued through socialization involuntarily demonstrated that even money, capital, and liquidity are not simply private goods held in private hands for private ends but a public good, one that concerns and affects the entire citizenry. The effects of economic decision-making processes have themselves signaled the limits to the soundness of economic decisions.

Market and capital do not just form a coherent ensemble of economic forces; they are also a condensed sociopolitical power that dictates a code for formatting dependence structures in the social field. Whereas the adepts of economic neo-Scholasticism will continue to view the alliance of liberalism and capitalism as the real "metaphysics of the West,"[41] those of us who are interested in secularizing economic knowledge must set out to explain economies without invoking God, to interpret markets without relying on Providence, and to account for economic systems without assuming prestabilized harmonies.[42] So-called liberalism was never committed to an agenda of untrammeled freedom; rather, it was bound by providential commitments from which it derived its claim to a normative, norm-setting privilege. That is why the political question does not lie in the alternative between free markets and the dictates of the state, but in an economic agnosticism that recognizes the political dimension of political economy in the reduction of its eschatological rudiments and that distrusts the realization of practical reason through market forces.

Since it is one of the quirks of the capitalist economy that the consequences of its risky decision-making processes are felt even by those who have no say in them, and since risks differ from dangers in that the latter cannot be ascribed to our actions or inactions, it is clear that systemic economic risks and calculable damages have been transformed into elemental dangers for the dependent majority who are powerless to make decisions. Here the risks involved in the system's normal functioning surpass the limits of rational calculation, and it should probably come as no surprise that societies that operate in this way are "afraid of themselves."[43] "Financialization" processes have tied the reproduction of societies to the reproductive forms of capital. In a kind of large-scale experiment, the attempt has been made to adapt systems of social and political order to situations of economic risk. For that very reason, the possibility cannot be ruled out that the systematic financing promises we have undertaken have fettered us to a "perfidious future" (Keynes), with all the perils it brings. Automatic security mechanisms have produced a blindness to danger, and the commercialization of risk has made the potential damages infinitely costly or downright unaffordable.

Whereas modern welfare societies once emerged by transforming dangers into risks and by taming contingency, now danger and chance have returned in archaic form, as *týchē* or fortune, to wreak havoc at the center of societies: ungovernable, irregular, shapeless, and shrouded in ignorance. This much we know: competitive behavior on financial markets does not automatically tend to the common good. An interesting social model is not a helpful social program, and today's national economies will continue to be directly confronted with the question of whether—and how long—they can afford to finance their capitalist functional ideas and structures. If we contend that the unique character of capital becomes universal in finance capital, determining the life processes of society as a single force, then we must also conclude that the hazardous whims and caprices of age-old figures of sovereignty have returned under the most modern conditions. Here uncertainty has become arcane and decisions are made which, in their boundless lawlessness, have taken on the character of fate. That defines the contours of the current epoch of financial convulsions, the topography of the capitalist cosmopolis. It is the opaque and unstable fault zone into which our societies have financed themselves.

Notes

CHAPTER I

1. Don DeLillo, *Cosmopolis*, London 2004, 12; in the following discussion, quotations are taken from this edition and are acknowledged by page numbers in parentheses in the body of the text. Honoré de Balzac, "Das Bankhaus Nucingen" (The firm of Nucingen), in *Das Bankhaus Nucingen: Erzählungen*, Zürich 1977, 8; ibid., "Gobseck," 147, 155; Karl Marx, "The Means of Circulation under the Credit System," in *Capital*, vol. 3, trans. David Fernbach, London 2006, 667; Edward Chancellor, *Devil Take the Hindmost: A History of Financial Speculation*, New York 2000, 262, 265, cf. David Cowart, "Anxieties of Obsolescence: DeLillo's *Cosmopolis*," in *The Holodeck in the Garden: Science and Technology in Contemporary American Fiction*, ed. Peter Freese and Charles B. Harris, Normal, Ill. 2004, 179–91; Nick Heffernan, "Money Is Talking to Itself: Finance Capitalism in the Fiction of Don DeLillo from *Players* to *Cosmopolis*," *Critical Engagements: A Journal of Theory and Criticism* 1:2, 2007, 53–78; Per Serritslev Petersen, "Don DeLillo's *Cosmopolis* and the Dialectics of Complexity and Simplicity in Postmodern American Philosophy and Culture," *American Studies in Scandinavia* 37:2, 2005, 70–84; Jerry A. Varsava, "The Saturated Self: Don DeLillo on the Problem of Rogue-Capitalism," *Contemporary Literature* 46:1, 2005, 78–107.

2. Karl Marx and Friedrich Engels, *Manifesto of the Communist Party*, trans. Samuel Moore, ed. F. Bender, New York 1988, 54; Joseph Schumpeter, *Capitalism, Socialism and Democracy*, ch. 7, "The Process of Creative Destruction," London 1943, 81–86; Jean Baudrillard, *Symbolic Exchange and Death*, part 1, "The End of Production," London 1993, 6–49; Luc Boltanski and Eve Chiapello, *The New Spirit of Capitalism*, trans. Gregory Elliot, New York 2005; Jeremy Rifkin, *The Age of Access: How the Shift from Ownership to Access Is Transforming Capitalism*, London 2001, 30–55.

3. Stefan Altdorfer (ed.), *History of Financial Disasters: 1763–1995*, vol. 3, London 2006, 276–77.

4. G.W.F. Hegel, *Vorlesungen über Ästhetik III*, in *Werke*, vol. 15, Frankfurt/M. 1970, 340–41, 364, 378, 384; or see *Aesthetics: Lectures on Fine Art*, vol. 2, trans. T. M. Knox, Oxford 1975, 1092ff.

5. DeLillo, *Cosmopolis*, 56, 152, 192. For the psychiatric classification of "amok," "hwa-byung," and "susto," see the *Diagnostic and Statistical Manual of Mental Disorders* (DSM-IV-TR), app. 1, "Outline for Cultural Formation and Glossary of Culture-Bound Syndromes," Washington 2000.

6. Joel Kurtzman, *The Death of Money: How the Electronic Economy Has Destabilized the World's Markets and Created Financial Chaos*, New York 1993, 17; Rifkin, *Age of Access*, ch. 3.

7. See comments by the trader and mathematician Nicholas Taleb in *Fooled by Randomness: The Hidden Role of Chance in the Markets and in Life*, New York 2004, 103.

8. Nassim Nicholas Taleb, *The Black Swan: The Impact of the Highly Improbable*, New York 2007, xvii–xviii.

9. Jacques Attali, *La Crise et après*, Paris 2009.

10. See Justin Fox, *The Myth of the Rational Market: A History of Risk, Reward and Delusion on Wall Street*, New York 2009, xi–xii.

11. After the crash of 1997 it was calculated that, in a world in which price fluctuations display a standard statistical distribution, this event would have to be accorded a probability ratio of 10^{-16}; investors could therefore expect it to recur in the future after several billion times a billion years (cf. Fox, *Myth of the Rational Market*, 233). See also Paul Krugman, *The Accidental Theorist*, New York 1998, 158; Robert Brenner, *Boom and Bubble: The US in the World Economy*, New York and London 2003, 279.

12. See Paul Krugman, "How Did Economists Get It so Wrong?" *New York Times*, Sept. 2, 2009.

13. Daniel Defoe, "The Anatomy of Exchange Alley" (1719), in *Political and Economic Writings of Daniel Defoe*, vol. 6, *Finance*, ed. John McVeah, London 2000, 129–56; Charles MacKay, *Extraordinary Popular Delusions and the Madness of Crowds* (1841/1852), New York 1980; Robert J. Shiller, *Irrational Exuberance*, Princeton 2005. Cf. Urs Stäheli, *Spectacular Speculation: Thrills, the Economy and Popular Discourse*, trans. Eric Savoth, Stanford 2013.

14. M.F.M. Osborne, *The Stock Market and Finance from a Physicist's Viewpoint*, vol. 1, *Market Making and Random Walks in Security Data*, Temple Hills/Madison 1977, 4, 22, passim.

15. Michael Henochsberg, *La place du marché. Essai*, Paris 2001, 212–15.

16. Robert B. Edwards and John Magee, *Technical Analysis of Stock Trends* (1947), Springfield 1961, 1–11; Fox, *Myth of the Rational Market*, 68; John J. Murphy, *Intermarket Technical Analysis: Trading Strategies for the Global Stock, Bond, Commodity and Currency Markets*, New York 1991, 39, 275ff; Friedrich Nagler, *Timing-Probleme am Aktienmarkt: Ein Vergleich von Strategien der Random Walk Hypothese, der Formelanlageplanung und der technischen Analyse*, Cologne 1979, 25ff.

17. See Benoit B. Mandelbrot and Richard L. Hudson, *The (Mis)Behaviour of Markets: A Fractal View of Risk, Ruin and Reward*, London 2008.

18. Immanuel Kant, "On the Miscarriage of All Philosophical Trials in Theodicy," trans. Allen W. Wood and George Di Giovanni, in *Religion within the Boundaries of Mere Reason and Other Writings*, Cambridge 1998, 17–18.

19. The term "oikodicy"—coined by the author—is modeled on the Greek term "theodicy," literally "God's justice." In post-Reformation Europe theodicy referred to a Christian worldview, according to which divine Providence was the guiding force in human society. In the late seventeenth century this belief was interpreted metaphysically by Leibniz, who asserted that the result of divine Providence was "the best of all possible worlds." The author's term "oikodicy" identifies a later development in which the market economy itself assumes the role of providence in shaping a just social order. —*Translators' note.*

CHAPTER 2

1. Thomas Hobbes, *Philosophical Rudiments Concerning Government and Society*, ed. Howard Warrender, Oxford 1983, 32.

2. Peter Sloterdijk, *Im Weltinnenraum des Kapitals. Für eine philosophische Theorie der Globalisierung*, Frankfurt/M. 2005, 79.

3. See Immanuel Kant, "Idea for a Universal History with a Cosmopolitan Purpose," in *Political Writings*, ed. H. S. Reiss, Cambridge 1991, 44; see also Kant, "Perpetual Peace: A Philosophical Sketch," ibid., 112; Samuel Pufendorf, *Die Gemeinschaftspflichten des Naturrechts. Ausgewählte Stücke aus "De officio Hominis et Civis"* (1673), Frankfurt/M. 1943, 9ff.

4. Bernard Mandeville, *The Fable of the Bees: or, Private Vices, Public Benefits*, ed. F. B. Kaye, Oxford 1924, 106.

5. On this and the following, see Albert O. Hirschman, *The Passions and the Interests.* Princeton: 1997, 14–55; Michel Foucault, *The Birth of Biopolitics. Lectures at the Collège de France 1978–1979*, trans. Graham Burchell, New York: 2008, 44–47.

6. Claude Adrien Helvetius, *De l'esprit*, Paris 1758, 53: "*Si l'univers physique est soumis aux lois du mouvement, l'univers moral ne l'est pas moins à celle de l'intérêt.*"

7. Johannes Sambacus, *Emblemata et aliquot nummi operis*, Antwerp 1566 (Reprint: Hildesheim et al. 2002), 139 (with thanks to Jason Papadimas for this reference).

8. Amartya Sen, "Rational Fools: A Critique of the Behavioral Foundations of Economic Theory," in *The Self and the Political Order*, ed. Tracy B. Strong, New York 1992, 121.

9. Immanuel Kant, "Anthropologie in pragmatischer Hinsicht," in *Werke*, vol. 6, 17.

10. Cf. Isaak Iselin, *Versuch über gesellige Ordnung*, Basel 1772, 63: Providence has arranged things in such a way that out of the struggle for "different advantages, general wellbeing arises."

11. Adam Smith, *Enquiry into the Nature and Causes of the Wealth of Nations*, vol. 2, ed. William Playfair, London 1995, 190.

12. Joseph Glanvill, *The Vanity of Dogmatizing: or Confidence in Opinions. Manifested in a Discourse of the Shortness and Uncertainty of Our Knowledge, and Its Causes; With Some Reflections on Peripateticism; and an Apology for Philosophy*, London 1661, 179–80, cited in Stefan Andriopoulos, "The Invisible Hand: Supernatural Agency in Political Economy and the Gothic Novel," *ELH* 66, 1999, 741 (the following reflections refer back to this essay).

13. Adam Smith, "The Principles Which Lead and Direct Philosophical Enquiries: Illustrated by the History of Astronomy," in *The Early Writings*, New York 1967, 48–49, cited in Andriopoulos, "Invisible Hand," 740; cf. Syed Ahmad, "Adam Smith's Four Invisible Hands," *History of Political Economy* 22:1, 1990, 137–44. On the theological origin and Providentialism of the "invisible hand," cf. Giorgio Agamben, *Herrschaft und Herrlichkeit. Zur theologischen Genealogie von Ökonomie und Regierung*, Frankfurt/M. 2010, 332–42.

14. Adam Smith, *Theory of Moral Sentiments*, ed. Knud Haakonssen, Cambridge 2002, 215–16.

15. Johann Wolfgang von Goethe, *Wilhelm Meisters Lehrjahre*, in *Werke*, vol. 7, ed. E. Trunz, Munich 1981, 388–93.

16. Julius Graf von Soden, *Die National-Ökonomie. Ein philosophischer Versuch über die Quellen des National-Reichtums, und über die Mittel zu dessen Beförderung*, vol. 3, Leipzig 1808, 6; Johann Georg Büsch, *Abhandlung von dem Geldumlauf in anhaltender Rücksicht auf die Staatswirtschaft und Handlung*, vol. 1, Hamburg et al. 1780, 173.

17. Charles-Louis de Montesquieu, *The Spirit of the Laws*, ed. A. Cohler et al., Cambridge 1989, 338. Cf. Karl Marx: "In the tender annals of political economy, the idyllic reigns from time immemorial." *Capital*, vol. 1, trans. Ben Fowkes, Harmondsworth 1976, 784.

18. Milton Friedman, "Free to Choose," cited in Pierre Rosanvallon, *Le libéralisme économique. Histoire de l'idée du marché*, Paris 1989; Friedman, *Capitalism and Freedom*, Chicago 1982, 13, 133.

19. François Quesnay, "Droit naturel," cited in Louis Dumont, *Homo aequalis. Genèse et épanouissement de l'idéologie économique*, Paris 1977, 53; Georg Andreas Will, *Versuch über die Physiokratie*, Nuremberg 1782, 3.

20. Foucault, *Birth of Biopolitics*, 61–62, 120.

21. Ferdinando Galiani, *De la monnaie* (1751), ed. G. H. Bousquet and J. Crisafulli, Paris 1955, 65; see also *Dialogues sur la commerce des bleds*, London 1770, 145, 235–36.

22. Anne-Robert Jacques Turgot, "Réflexions sur la formation et la distribution des richesses," in *Écrits économiques*, Paris 1970, 123ff; David Hume, *Political Discourses*, 2nd ed., Edinburgh 1752, 53, 93–94; Galiani, *Dialogues*, 145.

23. See Horst Claus Rechtenwald, "Würdigung des Werks," in Smith, *Wohlstand der Nationen, LVI*, for praise of the "beauty" of Smith's system; see also Friedrich August von Hayek, *The Trend of Economic Thinking: Essays on Political Economists and Economic History*, in *Collected Works of F.A. Hayek*, vol. 3, Indianapolis 1991, 120.

24. Adam Smith, *An Inquiry into the Nature and Causes of the Wealth of Nations*, ed. R. H. Campbell and A. S. Skinner, vol. 1, Oxford 1976, 72– 81, esp. 77.

25. Jean-Claude Perrot, *Une histoire intellectuelle de l'économie politique (XVIIe-XVIIIe siècles)*, Paris 1992, 245; Kenneth J. Arrow, *General Equilibrium*, Oxford 1983, 107–32. On the relationship between analytical mechanics and political economy, see M. Norton Wise, "Work and Waste: Political Economy and Natural Philosophy in Nineteenth Century Britain (I)," *History of Science* 27, 1989, 274–75.

26. Rosanvallon, *Libéralisme Économique*, 41, 70.

CHAPTER 3

1. See Karl Pribram, *A History of Economic Reasoning*, Baltimore 1983, 605–7, 612–14; "The Rise and Fall of the Concept of Equilibrium in Economic Analysis," in *Recherches Economiques de Louvain* 55:4, 1989, 447–68.

2. Kenneth J. Arrow and F. H. Hahn, *General Competitive Analysis*, San Francisco 1971, vi–vii; Milton Friedman, "The Methodology of Positive Economics," in *The Essence of Friedman*, ed. Kurt K. Leube, Stanford 1987, 154–56. On the subject of the "economy" of economic discourse, cf. Jakob Tanner, "Kultur in den Wirtschaftswissenschaften und kulturwissenschaftliche Interpretationen ökonomischen Handelns," in *Handbuch der Kulturwissenschaften. Themen und Tendenzen*, vol. 3, ed. Friedrich Jaeger, Jörn Rüsen, et al., Stuttgart 2004, 203, 220.

3. Andreas Langenohl, *Finanzmarkt und Temporalität. Imaginäre Zeit und kulturelle Repräsentation der Gesellschaft*, Stuttgart 2007, 82–86.

4. Immanuel Kant, "The Contest of Faculties," in *Kant: Political Writings*, ed. H. S. Reiss, Cambridge 1991, 177.

5. On this and the following point see Friedrich A. von Hayek, *Der Wettbewerb als Entdeckungsverfahren*, Kiel 1968; on Hayek's concept of catallaxy (from Greek *katallatein*, to exchange, trade, admit into the community), cf. Philip Batthyány, *Zwang als Grundübel der Gesellschaften?* Tübingen 2007, 32–34.

6. According to the Ricardo follower James R. McCullough, *The Principles of Political Economy*, Edinburgh 1825, cited in Wise, "Work and Waste" (I), 277.

7. Cf. Foucault, *Birth of Biopolitics*, 120–21; on the relationship between economic theory (especially in the Freiburg School) and Husserl's eidetic reduction, see ibid., 128.

8. Friedman, "Methodology of Positive Economics," 154.

9. See Philip Mirowski et al., *More Heat than Light: Economics as Social Physics, Physics as Nature's Economics*, Cambridge/MA 1989; *Machine Dreams: Economics Becomes a Cyborg Science*, Cambridge/MA et al. 2002; Wise, "Work and Waste" (I–II), *History of Science* 27, 1989, 263–301, 392–449; Fox, *Myth of the Rational Market*, 6–10; Pribram, *History of Economic Reasoning*, 277–83, 285–89, 308–13; Osborne, *Stock Market from a Physicist's Viewpoint*; Joseph Vogl, "Kreisläufe," in *Transfusionen. Blutbilder und Biopolitik in der Neuzeit*, ed. Anja Lauper et al., Berlin 2005, 99–118.

10. F.S.C. Northrop, "The Impossibility of a Theoretical Science of Economic Dynamics," *Quarterly Journal of Economics* 56:1, Nov. 1941, 1–17; Mirowski, "Rise and Fall of the Concept of Equilibrium," 449–52.

11. Arrow and Hahn, *General Competitive Analysis*, v; cf. Franklin M. Fisher et al., *Disequilibrium Foundations of Equilibrium Economics*, Cambridge/MA 1983, 3–5.

12. Cf. George Soros, *The Crisis of Global Capitalism. Open Society Endangered*, Berlin 1998; Robert Shiller, cited in Fox, *Myth of the Rational Market*, 232; János Korani et al., *Anti-Equilibrium. On Economic Systems Theory and the Tasks of Research*, Amsterdam 1971, xv–xvi; Jacques Sapir, *Les trous noirs de la science économique. Essaie sur l'impossibilité de penser le temps de l'argent*, Paris 2000, 45ff.

13. Henri Pirenne, *Sozial-und Wirtschaftsgeschichte Europas im Mittelalter*, Bern 1947, 117ff; Michael North et al. (eds.), *Kredit im spätmittelalterlichen frühneuzeitlichen Europa*, Cologne 1991; Michael Hutter, *The Emergence of Bank Notes in the 17th Century* (typescript).

14. Joseph Addison, *The Spectator*, ed. D. F. Bond, Oxford 1965, 14–17.

15. Cf. Helma Houtman De Smendt and Hermann van der Wee, "Die Geschichte des modernen Geld- und Finanzwesens Europas in der Neuzeit," in *Europäische Bankengeschichte*, ed. Hans Pohl, Frankfurt/M. 1993, 153–63; Eva Schumann-Bacia, *Die Bank von England und ihr Architekt John Soane*, Zurich 1989, 29–31.

16. Anon., "Entwurf der Ephemeriden der Menschheit," in *Ephemeriden der Menschheit oder Bibliothek der Sittenlehre und der Politik* 1 (1776), 2; cf. William Petty, *The Economic Writings*, vol. 2, Cambridge/MA 1899, 446.

17. Daniel Defoe, "An Essay on Public Credit" (1710), in *Political and Economic Writings*, ed. W. R. Owens and P. N. Furbank, vol. 6, *Finance*, ed. John McVeagh, London 2000, 53–56. On the relationship between monetary symbols, underlying value, circulation, and balance in the monetary theories of the Enlightenment, cf. Joseph Vogl, *Kalkül und Leidenschaft: Poetik des ökonomischen Menschen*, Berlin et al. 2009, 120–23, 224–33 (the following account draws a great deal upon this work).

18. Anon., *Geschichte der Bank von England von ihrer Entstehung bis auf den heutigen Tag*, Bremen 1797, 1, 43, 48, 80; David Ricardo, *On the Principles of Political Economy and Taxation*, London, John Murray 1817 (for Jean Baptiste Say's remark); Henry Thornton, *An Enquiry into the Nature and Effects of the Paper Credit of Great Britain* (1802), ed. F. von Hayek, London 1939 and New York 1965, 65–277.

19. Joseph Alois Schumpeter, *Geschichte der ökonomischen Analyse*, Göttingen 1965, 406.

20. Adam Müller, *Elemente der Staatskunst*, vol. 1, ed. J. Baxa, Leipzig 1922, 434–35. Cf. Adam Müller, "Londoner Bank," in *Allgemeine deutsche Realenzyklopädie für die gebildeten Stände (Conversations-Lexikon)*, vol. 6, Leipzig 1827, 656–61.

21. According to Napoleon's later adviser and banker Count von Mollien, cited in Charles Rist, *History of Monetary and Credit Theories from John Laws to the Present Day*, trans. Jane Degras, London 1940, 91 (translation modified).

22. Anon., "Über den neuesten Finanzzustand Frankreichs," *Berlinische Monatsschrift* 16, 1790, 8. Cf. anon., *Examen comparatif des deux mondes. Proposés pour liquider la dette, les quittances, ou les assignats*, Paris 1790, 16; Marie Jean Antoine Condorcet, *Sur la proposition d'acquitter la dette exigible en assignats*, Paris 1790, 13f; Edmund Burke, *Discours sur la monnaie de papier et sur le système des assignats de France*, Paris 1790 (Sept.), 4, 11; François d'Ivernois, *Geschichte der französischen Finanzadministration im Jahr 1796*, trans. F. Gentz, Berlin 1797, xviii.

23. François Veron de Forbonnais, *Observations succinctes sur l'Emission de deux milliards d'Assignats territoriaux, avec un cours forcé de monnaie*; Edmund Burke, *Discours sur la monnaie de papier*, 4f; Antoine Laurent de Lavoisier, *Réflexions sur les Assignats et sur la liquidation de la dette exigible ou arrièrée*, 11. For an interpretation of this monetary policy in the light of the law of proportion and quantity theory, see Julian Borchardt, *Das Papiergeld in der Revolution 1797–1920*, Berlin 1921, 20.

24. According to the finance specialist Baron de Cernon in a speech on the issuing of banknotes given in November 1789, cited in Jean Morini-Comby, *Les Assignats. Révolutions et inflation*, Paris 1925, 16f; cf. Marie Jean Antoine Condorcet, *Nouvelles réflexions sur le projet de payer la dette exigible en papier forcé*, 1ff.

25. Edmund Burke, *Reflections on the Revolution in France*, ed. J.G.A. Pocock, Indianapolis 1987, 166–174; *Sur la proposition d'acquitter la dette exigible en assignats*, 31ff; d'Ivernois, *Geschichte der französischen Finanzadministration*, xx.

26. Henry Thornton, *An Enquiry into the Nature and Effects of the Paper Credit of Great Britain*, London 1802, Reprints of Economics Classics, New York 1965, 139.

27. Karl Munk, *Zur Geschichte und Theorie der Banknote mit besonderer Rücksicht auf die Lehren der klassischen Nationalökonomie*, Bern 1896, 44ff.

28. Johann Friedrich Reitmeier, *Neues System des Papiergeldes und des Geldwesens beim Gebrauch des Papiergeldes in zwei Abhandlungen*, Kiel 1814, 34f.

29. Friedrich Gentz, "Über die österreichische Bank," in *Schriften*, vol. 3/2, ed. G. Schlesier, Mannheim 1839, 297; Thornton, *Paper Credit*, New York 1965, 125, 126; on the emergence of the first credit theories, cf. Rist, *Geschichte der Geld-und Kredittheorien*, 346; and on the "new era" of money theories marked by Thornton, cf. Hayek, *Trend of Economic Thinking*, 321.

30. Adam Müller, *Versuche einer neuen Theorie des Geldes mit besonderer Rücksicht auf Großbrittanien*, Leipzig and Altenberg 1816, 87; cf. Talcott Parsons, *Zur Theorie der sozialen Interaktionsmedien*, ed. S. Jensen, Opladen 1980, 98ff; Niklas Luhmann, *Die Wirtschaft der Gesellschaft*, Frankfurt/M. 1994, 134.

31. Thornton, *Paper Credit*, New York 1965, 231.

32. Rist, *Geschichte der Geld-und Kredittheorien*, 85f.

33. Cf. Daniel Defoe, *The Chimera: or, The French Way of Paying National Debts Laid Open*, London 1720, 6; John Vernon, *Money and Fiction: Literary Realism in the Nineteenth and Early Twentieth Century*, Ithaca and London 1984, 17f, 37.

34. Müller, *Elemente der Staatskunst*, vol. 1, 353. Cf. Ethel Matala de Mazza, *Der verfasste Körper. Zum Projekt einer organischen Gemeinschaft in der Politischen Romantik*, Freiburg 1999, 331–39.

35. Marx, *Das Kapital*, vol. 1, in *MEW*, vol. 23, 782, 163–67; Rudolph Hilferding, *Das Finanzkapital. Eine Studie über jüngste Entwicklung des Kapitalismus*, Berlin 1955, 62–68; Fredric Jameson, "Culture and Finance Capital," *Critical Inquiry* 24:1, 1997, 264–65. On the saleability of debts and associated financial innovations, which can already be traced back to the financing of state debts in the sixteenth-century Netherlands, cf. Altdorfer (ed.), *History of Financial Disasters*, xxvii.

36. Adam Müller, *Elemente der Staatskunst*, vol. 1, 435, vol. 2, 104–5; "Versuche einer neuen Theorie des Geldes," 97; "Zeitgemäße Betrachtungen über den Geldumlauf (1816)," in *Ausgewählte Abhandlungen*, ed. J. Baxa, Jena 1931, 55; Thornton, *Paper Credit*, New York 1965, 30ff. Here one could speak of the fictional acts or enabling fictions with which finance capitalism is instituted; cf. Andreas Langenohl, "Die Sinndimensionen der Markt-Zeit. Zum Verhältnis zwischen der Operationsweise von Finanzmärkten und ihren (Selbst-) Darstellungen," in *Die Markt-Zeit in der Finanzwirtschaft: Soziale, kulturelle und ökonomische Dimensionen*, ed. Andreas Langenohl and Kerstin Schmidt-Beck, Marburg 2007, 2.

37. On the ways in which not only classical concepts of balance, but also the status of economic or, rather, empirical knowledge is itself problematized by such factors as time, expectancy, and future uncertainty, cf. Friedrich A. von Hayek, "Economics and Knowledge," *Economica*, New Series 4:13, Feb. 1934, 33–54.

CHAPTER 4

1. This relates in particular to the "banking/currency" controversy that has determined the choreography of financial-political debates since the midnineteenth century; cf. John Hicks, *Critical Essays in Monetary Theory*, Oxford 1967, vii–viii.

2. Cf. the assessment by Fred L. Block et al., *The Origins of International Economic Disorder: A Study of United States International Monetary Policy from World War II to the Present*, Berkeley 1977, 5–6.

3. Cf. Chancellor, *Devil Take the Hindmost*, 236; Filippo Cesarano, *Monetary Theory and Bretton Woods: The Construction of an International Monetary Order*, Cambridge/MA 2006, x; Richard Tilly, *Geld und Kredit in der Wirtschaftsgeschichte*, Stuttgart 2003, 190; Milton Friedman, *The Essence of Friedman*, 379, 501.

4. Cf. Barry Eichengreen, *Globalizing Capital: A History of the International Monetary System*, Princeton 1996, 49–50; Angela Redish, "Anchors Aweigh: The Transition from Commodity Money to Fiat Money in Western Economics," *Canadian Journal of Economics* 26:4, Nov. 1993, 777–95.

5. Standing in for the extensive literature on this subject, see A.L.K. Acheson et al. (eds.), *Bretton Woods Revisited. Evaluations of the International Monetary Fund and the International Bank for Reconstruction and Development*, Toronto 1972; Eichengreen, *Globalizing Capital*; Barry Eichengreen, *Global Imbalances and the Lessons of Bretton Woods*, Cambridge/MA 2007; Block, *Origins of Economic Disorder*, 193–99; Richard Tilly, *Geld und Kredit in der Wirtschaftsgeschichte*, Stuttgart 2003, 186–94; Brenner, *Boom and Bubble*, 41–63; Cesarano, *Monetary Theory*.

6. Friedman, *Essence of Friedman*, 501. On "the postmodern rupture" of this economy, see Jean Joseph Goux, "Spéculations fatales. La crise économique de 2008," *Esprit* 350, Dec. 2008, 45; Cesarano, *Monetary Theory*, ix, 189; David Harvey, *The Condition of Postmodernity: An Enquiry into the Origins of Cultural Change*, Oxford 1989, 121ff.

7. Milton Friedman, "The Need for Futures Markets in Currencies," in *The Futures Market in Foreign Currencies: Papers by Milton Friedman [and others]; Prepared for the International Monetary Market of the Chicago Mercantile Exchange*, Chicago 1972, 6–12. Cf. Milton Friedman et al., *Essays in Positive Economics*, Chicago 1966, 176; Milton Friedman, *Capitalism and Freedom*, Chicago 1962, 67ff; Robert V. Roosa, *The Balance of Payments: Free versus Fixed Exchange Rates*, Washington 1967, 14–20; *Essence of Friedman*, 461–98.

8. Dick Bryan and Michael Rafferty, *Capitalism with Derivatives: A Political Economy of Financial Derivatives, Capital and Class*, New York 2006, 133.

9. Cf. Edward Li Puma, Benjamin Lee, et al., *Financial Derivatives and the Globalization of Risk*, Durham 2004, 16, 47, 61; Donald MacKenzie, *An Engine*,

Not a Camera: How Financial Models Shape Markets, Cambridge/MA et al. 2006, 145–50.

10. Merton H. Miller, *Merton Miller on Derivatives*, New York 1997, ix–x, 68, 87; Friedman, *Capitalism and Freedom*, 67 ff.; *Essence of Friedman*, 419.

11. Joseph de la Vega, *Die Verwirrungen der Verwirrungen* (1688), ed. Otto Pringsheim, Breslau 1919, 23–30, 136–40; Isaak Pinto, *Traité des fonds de commerce, ou jeu d'actions*, London 1772, 282–304. Cf. Chancellor, *Devil Take the Hindmost*, 21; Brian Rotman, *Signifying Nothing: The Semiotics of Zero*, London 1987, 150.

12. Pierre-Joseph Proudhon, *Manuel du spéculateur à la Bourse*, Paris 1857, 36.

13. Cf. Stäheli, *Spectacular Speculation*, 72–75; Marieke de Goede et al., *Virtue, Fortune and Faith: A Genealogy of Finance*, Minneapolis 2005, 47–50; Fox, *Myth of the Rational Market*, 39–40; Chancellor, *Devil Take the Hindmost*, 246.

14. Max Weber, "Stock and Commodity Exchanges," trans. Steven Lestition, *Theory and Society* 29:3, 2000, 309–10; cf. Stäheli, *Spectacular Speculation*, 68–70.

15. Samuel Weber et al., *Geld ist Zeit. Gedanken zu Kredit und Krise*, Berlin 2009. On speculative "destruction," cf. Georg Wilhelm Friedrich Hegel, *Differenz des Fichteschen und Schllingschen Systems der Philosophie* (1801), in *Werke*, vol. 2, Frankfurt/M. 1986, 34.

16. Cf. Elena Esposito, *Die Zukunft der Futures. Die Zeit des Geldes in Finanzwelt und Gesellschaft*, Heidelberg 2010, 110, 172–74. Max Weber had already insisted that the mechanism of futures trading must be explained through the logic of credit transfer; cf. Weber, "Stock and Commodity Exchanges," 305–38.

17. See Miller, *Merton Miller on Derivatives*, 80–83.

18. Eugene Fama and Merton H. Miller, *The Theory of Finance*, Hinsdale 1972, 335–36ff.

19. Pierre Legendre, *Le désir politique de dieu. Etude sur les montages de l'État et du Droit, Leçons VII*, Paris 1988, 101–2; on the relationship between Providence, efficiency, and the capitalist "spirit" of Protestantism, see Manfred Schneider, *Das Attentat. Kritik der paranoischen Vernunft*, Berlin 2010, 182–92.

20. Louis Bachelier, *Théorie de la spéculation. Annales scientifiques de l'École Normale Supérieure*, ser. 3, vol. 17, 1900, 21–86; John Cassidy, *How Markets Fail. The Logic of Economic Calamities*, New York 2009, 86–90.

21. Paul Samuelson, cited in Burton G. Malkiel, *A Random Walk Down Wall Street*, New York 2003, 187, 196–97; cf. Fama and Miller, *Theory of Finance*, 339–40; Paul A. Samuelsen, "Proof That Properly Anticipated Prices Fluctuate Randomly" (1965), in *Collected Scientific Papers of Paul A. Samuelsen*, vol. 3, Cambridge/MA et al. 1972, 782–90; Jürg Niehans, *A History of Economic Theory: Classical Contributions 1729–1980*, Baltimore et al. 1990, 441–42.

22. On this and the Black-Scholes-Merton models in general, see Esposito, *Die Zukunft der Futures*, 189–215; Nicholas Dunbar, *Inventing Money: The Story*

of Long-Term Capital Management and the Legends Behind It, Chichester 2000, passim; MacKenzie, *Engine, Not a Camera*, 119–78; de Goede, *Virtue, Fortune and Faith*, 125–32. The fundamental publications are Fischer Black and Myron Scholes, "The Pricing of Options and Corporate Liabilities," *Journal of Political Economy* 81, May/June 1973, 637–54; Robert C. Merton, *Theory of Rational Option Pricing*, Cambridge/MA 1971.

23. In this regard we refer not only to the judgment of Bachelier (1900) but also to the "Theorie der Prämierengeschäfte" (1908) by the Boltzmann student and political mathematician Vincenzo Bronzin; cf. Wolfgang Hafner, "Ein vergessener genialer Wurf zur Bewertung von Optionen. Vinzenz Bronzin nahm die nobelpreiswürdige Black/Scholes Formel vorweg," *NZZ*, Oct. 8, 2005, "Fokus der Wissenschaft."

24. See Robert C. Merton, *Continuous-Time Finance*, Cambridge/MA 1990, 15.

25. MacKenzie, *Engine, Not a Camera*, 20, 158, 174; Li Puma et al. *Financial Derivatives*, 38, 60–61; Esposito, *Die Zukunft der Futures*, 136, 203; Randy Martin, "The Twin Towers of Financialization: Entanglements of Political and Cultural Economies," *Global South* 3:1, Spring 2009, 119.

26. Patrice Flichy, "The Birth of Long Distance Communication: Semaphore Telegraphs in Europe (1790–1840)," *Réseaux* 1:1, 1993, 96–100 (with thanks to Anders Engberg-Pedersen for this reference). Cf. in general Stäheli, *Spektakuläre Spektakulation*, 305–63; Ramon Reichert, *Das Wissen der Börse. Medien und Praktiken des Fianazmarktes*, Bielefeld 2009.

27. B. Mandelbrot and R. L. Hudson, *The (Mis)Behavior of Markets*. New York: 2008, 254.

28. Merton, *Continuous-Time Finance*, 470; cf. Reichert, *Das Wissen der Börse*, 113–14, 217.

29. The title of a 1999 BBC documentary on the fate of the Black-Scholes formula; cf. http://www.bbc.co.uk/science/horizon/1999/midas.shtml (accessed on July 5, 2010).

30. S. Ross, "Finance," in *The New Palgrave Dictionary of Economics*, ed. J. Eatwell et al., vol. 2, London 1987, 332, cited in Esposito, *Die Zukunft der Futures*, 204.

31. Cf. Chancellor, *Devil Take the Hindmost*, 237–38; Cesarano, *Monetary Theory*, 208–9. The most recent and controversial version of high-frequency trading involves the practice of "flash orders," where advances in the speed of calculation are used to test the market by issuing and annulling purchase orders almost simultaneously (cf. Jenny Anderson, "S.E.C. Moves to Ban Edge Held by Fast Traders," *New York Times*, Sept. 18, 2008, 1, 3).

32. Fischer Black, cited in Dunbar, *Inventing Money*, 33, cf. 91.

33. Robert C. Merton and an unnamed broker in interviews cited in de Goede, *Virtue, Fortune and Faith*, 131.

34. James Yorke, cited in James Gleick, *Chaos: Making a New Science*, London 1987, 67–68.

35. Robert C. Merton, "Application of Option-Pricing Theory: Twenty-Five Years Later," *American Economic Review* 88:3, June 1998, 324, 336; Arrow, *General Equilibrium Theory*. Cf. de Goede, *Virtue, Fortune and Faith*, 140.

36. Robert J. Shiller, *The New Financial Order. Risk in the 21st Century*, Princeton 2003, 1–2.

37. Ibid., 6, 16–17.

38. Ibid., 2–3, 15.

39. James Glassman and Kevin Hassett, *Dow 36,000*, New York 2000, 20–37.

40. See the various reports from the Clinton administration and by Alan Greenspan in 1997, cited in Chancellor, *Devil Take the Hindmost*, 230.

41. Francis Fukuyama, *The End of History and the Last Man*, New York 1992/3, 14, 371; cf. Jacques Derrida, *Specters of Marx: The State of the Debt, the Work of Mourning and the New International*, trans. Peggy Kamuf, New York 1994, 70–72, 74–79, 82–86. It may, however, be no coincidence that earlier discussions of posthistorical modernization referred explicitly to prominent theorists of economic equilibrium. Arnold Gehlen claimed to have discovered the concept of "post-history" in Antoine Augustine Cournot and the concept of "crystallization" in Vinfredo Pareto—economists to whom the first formalizations of economic balancing processes as well as the socio-philosophical reshaping of those processes can be attributed. With this move, posthistorical decades were prophesied for the late twentieth century, which was said to be destined to "incessant activity" and "movement on a stationary basis." However cheerily or gloomily the end of historical time may have been imagined, there is some cause for assuming an epistemo-historical overlap between the many and varied views expressed about an end of history, on the one hand, and liberal ideas about how the economy functions, on the other (cf. Arnold Gehlen, "Ende der Geschichte?" in *Einblicke*, Frankfurt/M. 1975, 115–33; for discussion of "post-historical modernization" and the discovery of the concept of "post-history" by the mathematician and economist Cournot, cf. Lutz Niethammer, *Posthistoire. Has History Come to an End?* trans. Patrick Camiller, London 1994; and on mathematical equilibrium models in Cournot and Pareto, cf. Pribram, *History of Economic Reasoning*, 194–96, 308–13).

CHAPTER 5

1. See Greta Krippner, *The Fictitious Economy: Financialization, the State, and Contemporary Capitalism*, diss. Madison 2003; Gerald Epstein (ed.), *Financialization and the World Economy*, Cheltenham 2005; Martin, "Twin Towers of Financialization," 108–25.

2. Aristotle, *Politics*, 1252a–1253a.

3. Aristotle, *Politics*, 1256b.36–39, 1257a.15–32, 1323a.25–30; *Nichomachean Ethics*, 1129a.3–1133b.28. See also Arnaud Bertoud, *Aristote et l'Argent*, Paris 1981, 35; Richard F. Crespo, "The Ontology of 'the Economic': an Aristotelian Analysis," *Cambridge Journal of Economics* 30, 2006, 767–81; João César das Neves, "Aquinas and Aristotle's Distinction of Wealth," *History of Political Economy* 32:3, 2000, 649–57; Skip Worden, "Aristotle's Natural Wealth: The Role of Limitation in Thwarting Misordered Concupiscence," *Journal of Business Ethics* 84, 2009, 209–19.

4. Aristotle, *Politics*, 1256b.40–1257b.40; see W. L. Newman, *The Politics of Aristotle*, vol. 1: *Introduction to the Politics*, Salem/NH 1887 (Reprint: Salem/NH 1985), 127ff.

5. Aristotle, *Politics*, 1253b.15, 1256b.40ff, 1258a.37; see Pierre Pelegrin, "Monnaie et Chrématistique. Remarques sur le mouvement et le contenu de deux textes d'Aristote à l'occasion d'un livre récent," in *Revue Philosophique de la France et de l'étranger*, 1982/4, 631–44.

6. Aristotle, *Nichomachean Ethics*, 1129a.31–1129b.10, 1130a.15–36; *Politics*, 1253b.31–32. See also Peter Koslowski, "Haus und Geld. Zur aristotelischen Unterscheidung von Politik, Ökonomik und Chrematistik," *Philosophisches Jahrbuch* 86, 1979, 60–83; Arnaud Berthoud, *Essais de Philosophie économique. Platon, Hobbes, A. Smith, Marx*, Villeneuve-d'Ascq 2002, 72–79.

7. Aristotle, *Politics*, 1258b.4–8; see Plato, *Politeia*, 555e.

8. Berthoud, *Aristote et l'argent*, 178. See also Gilles Deleuze, *Differenz und Wiederholung*, Munich 1992, 121–22.

9. See Éric Alliez, "The Accident of Time: An Aristotelian Study," in *Capital Times. Tales from the Conquest of Time*, Minneapolis 1996, 1–24, esp. 2, 11–14.

10. Karl Polanyi, *Ökonomie und Gesellschaft*, Frankfurt/M. 1979, 149–85. See Plato, *Nomoi*, 704a–705b; Michael Austin and Pierre Vidal-Naquet, *Économies et societés en Grèce ancienne*, Paris 1972, 170–73; H. Bolkenstein, *Economic Life in Greece's Golden Age*, Leiden 1958, 105–6; M. I. Finley, *The Ancient Economy*, Berkeley 1973, 161–62; H. Knorriga, *Emporos. Data on Trade and Trader in Greek Literature from Homer to Aristotle*, Paris 1926, 9, 103.

11. Emile Benveniste, *Indo-European Language and Society*, London 1973, 113–20. On the economic history of emerging markets, see Karl Polanyi, *The Great Transformation. Politische und ökonomische Ursprünge von Gesellschaften und Wirtschaftssystemen*, Frankfurt/M. 1978, 87–101; Georges Duby, *Guerriers et paysans*, Paris 1973, 168; Henri Pirenne, *Les Villes au Moyen Âge. Essai d'histoire économique et sociale*, Paris 1992, 34–37; Henochsberg, *La Place du Marché*, 28ff.

12. From a moral sermon preached by Jacob of Vitry, cited in Jacques le Goff, *Your Money or Your Life: Economy and Religion in the Middle Ages*, New York

1990, 56–57. Le Goff's study may be consulted by readers interested in the variety of usurer figures and (anti-)usury laws in the Middle Ages.

13. Dante Alighieri, *The Divine Comedy*, Inferno 11, 49–50; William Shakespeare, *The Merchant of Venice*, I.3: In his first encounter with Antonio, Shylock compares his money-lending business with the lambs born of ewes and rams. Antonio counters, "Or is your gold and silver ewes and rams?" Shylock responds: "I cannot tell. I make it breed as fast." See LeGoff, *Your Money or Your Life*, 32; Pierre Dockès, "L'esprit du capitalisme, son histoire et sa crise," in Pierre Dockès et al., *Jours de colère. L'esprit du capitalisme*, Paris 2009, 99–101.

14. *Fortunatus*, ed. H.-G. Roloff, Stuttgart 1996; see Stephan L. Wales, "Potency in *Fortunatus*," *German Quarterly* 59, 1986, 5–18. Here alliances are frequently formed when streams of money "flow" into the "laps" of the women concerned.

15. Benjamin Franklin, "Advice to a Young Tradesman. Written from an Old One (12 July 1748)," in *The Autobiography and Other Writings on Politics, Economics, and Virtue*, ed. A. Houston, Cambridge/MA 2004, 200; see also Weber, *Geld ist Zeit*, 11–13.

16. Gilles Deleuze and Félix Guattari, *Anti-Oedipus*, trans. R. Hurley et al., London 2004, 245–48. This constellation is particularly relevant to the position of the family. In Aristotelian terms, it no longer prescribes the social form of "oikonomic" reproduction; rather, it becomes the form of a material that is subordinate to economic reproductions.

17. Marx, *Capital*, vol. 1, 171–72. See Langenohl, *Finanzmarkt und Temporalität*, 89; Deleuze and Guattari, *Anti-Oedipus*, 247–48.

18. Marx, *Capital*, vol. 1, 724.

19. Alexander Rüstow, in "Compte-rendu des séances du colloque Walter Lippmann" (Aug. 26–30, 1938), in *Travaux du Centre International d'Études pour la Rénovation du Libéralisme*, vol. 1, Paris 1939, 83 (cited in Foucault, *History of Governmentality*); Ludwig van Mises, *Human Action. A Treatise on Economics*, New Haven 1949, 2.

20. The concept is Rüstow's; see Foucault, *Birth of Biopolitics*, 148.

21. Ibid., 148.

22. Ibid., 148. See also Rifkin, *Access*, 10f.

23. Gary S. Becker, *The Essence of Becker*, ed. R. Ferrero and P. S. Schwartz, Stanford 1995, xxi; cf. Ingo Pies and Martin Leschke (eds.), *Beckers ökonomischer Imperialismus*, Tübingen 1998.

24. Michelle Riboud, *Accumulation du capital humaine*, Paris 1978, 1; see Burkhard Jaeger, *Humankapital und Unternehmenskultur. Ordnungspolitik für Unternehmen*, Wiesbaden 2004; Theodore W. Schultz, *In Menschen investieren. Die Ökonomik der Bevölkerungsqualität*, Tübingen 1986. At the same time, this is also one of the points of departure for Bourdieu's analysis of society in terms of

cultural and social capital; see Pierre Bourdieu, *Die verborgenen Mechanismen der Macht*, Hamburg 2005, 49–79.

25. G. Günter Voß and Hans J. Pongratz, "Die Arbeitskraftunternehmer. Eine neue Grundform der Ware Arbeit?" *Kölner Zeitschrift für Soziologie und Sozialpsychologie* 50, 1998, 131–58; Robert Johansen and Rob Swigart, *Upsizing the Individual in the Downsized Organization: Managing in the Wake of Reengineering, Globalization, and Overwhelming Technological Change*, Reading/MA 1994, 21ff. See also Dirk Baecker, *Postheroisches Management. Ein Vademecum*, Berlin 1994; Richard Sennett, *The Culture of the New Capitalism*, New Haven 2006; Nikolas Rose, "Tod des Sozialen? Eine Neubestimmung der Grenzen des Regierens," in *Gouvernementalität der Gegenwart. Studien zur Ökonomisierung des Sozialen*, ed. Ulrich Bröckling, Susanne Krasmann, and Thomas Lemke, Frankfurt/M. 2000, 72–109; Ulrich Bröckling, "Totale Mobilmachung. Menschenführung im Qualitäts- und Selbstmanagement," ibid., 131–67.

26. See, for example, William Bridges, *Creating You and Co: Learn to Think Like the CEO of Your Own Career*, London 1997; Conrad Seidel and Werner Beutelmeier, *Die Marke Ich. So entwickeln Sie Ihre persönliche Erfolgsstrategie!* Vienna 1999. Cf. David Harvey, *A Brief History of Neoliberalism*, Oxford 2005, 4.

27. Gary S. Becker, *The Economic Approach to Human Behavior*, Chicago 1976. See Foucault, *Birth of Biopolitics*; Jakob Tanner, "'Kultur' in den Wirtschaftswissenschaften und kulturwissenschaftliche Interpretationen menschlichen Handelns," 207–8.

28. Gary S. Becker, *A Treatise on the Family*, Cambridge/MA 1993, 7; cf. 155–56.

CHAPTER 6

1. Gilles Deleuze, "Sehen und Sprechen. Erfahrungen, Aussagen—Erinnerung an ein Denkexperiment," *Lettre International* 33, 1996, 87; "Begehren und Lust," in *Gilles Deleuze—Fluchtlinien der Philosophie*, ed. Friedrich Balke and Joseph Vogl, Munich 1996, 235; Deleuze and Guattari, *Anti-Oedipus*, 166.

2. Fernand Braudel, *Sozialgeschichte des 15.-18. Jahrhunderts*, Munich 1986, vol. 1: *Der Alltag*, 484; vol. 2, *Der Handel*, 438, 500–503.

3. See Hayek, *Trend of Economic Thinking*, 28; Northrop, "Impossibility of a Theoretical Science of Economic Dynamics," 1–10.

4. See, in particular, Benoit Mandelbrot, "Paretian Distribution and Income Maximization," *Quarterly Journal of Economics* 76, Feb. 1962, 57–85; "The Variation of Certain Speculative Prices," *Journal of Business* 36:4, Oct. 1963, 394–419; "New Methods in Statistical Economics," *Journal of Political Economy* 71:5, Oct. 1963, 421–40; "The Variation of Some Other Speculative Prices," *Journal of Business* 40:4, Jan. 1967, 393–413; "Statistical Methodology for Non-periodic

Cycles," *Annals of Economic and Social Measurement* 1, July 1972, 259–90. The following account is based heavily on Mirowski, "Rise and Fall of the Concept of Equilibrium in Economic Analysis"; Philip Mirowski, "From Mandelbrot to Chaos in Economic Theory," *Southern Economic Journal* 57:2, Oct. 1990, 289–307; Reichert, *Das Wissen der Börse*, 21–46.

   5. Mandelbrot, "Variation of Certain Speculative Prices," 394, 309. See David Kelsey, "The Economics of Chaos or the Chaos of Economics," *Oxford Economic Papers*, New Series 40:1, Mar. 1988, 2; Mandelbrot and Hudson, *(Mis)behavior of Markets*, 197–252.

   6. Ilya Prigogine and Isabelle Stengers, *Order out of Chaos. Man's New Dialogue with Nature*, Toronto 1984, 14, 140–44; Ilya Prigogine, *From Being to Becoming. Time and Complexity in the Physical Sciences*, San Francisco 1980, 131–50. See also Gleick, *Chaos*, 86–94; Reichert, *Das Wissen der Börse*, 36–40.

   7. Mandelbrot and Hudson, *(Mis)behavior of Markets*, 149; Mandelbrot, "Variation of Certain Speculative Prices," 415; "New Methods in Statistical Economics," 434; cf. Weissenfeld, Horst, and Stefan, *Im Rausch der Spekulation. Geschichten von Spiel und Spekulation aus vier Jahrhunderten*, Rosenheim 1999, 666.

   8. See Kelsey, "Economics of Chaos," 26.

   9. Joachim Peinke et al., "Turbulenzen am Finanzmarkt," *Einblicke. Mitteilungsblatt der Carl von Ossietzky Universität Oldenburg* 39, 18; cited in Reichert, *Das Wissen der Börse*, 43; see also ibid., 42.

   10. Mandelbrot, "New Methods in Statistical Economics," 433.

   11. These were complaints voiced by different representatives of "efficient market" theory like M. F. Osborne, Eugene Fama, and Paul Cootner, cited in Fox, *Myth of the Rational Market*, 134–35; see Mirowski, "Rise and Fall of the Concept of Equilibrium in Economic Analysis," 465. On "nomadic" science, see Gilles Deleuze and Félix Guattari, *A Thousand Plateaus. Capitalism and Schizophrenia*, trans. Brian Massumi, London 2004, 387–467.

   12. Deleuze and Guattari, *Anti-Oedipus*, 254. See also Ping Shen, "Empirical and Theoretical Evidence of Economic Chaos," *System Dynamics Review* 4:1–2, 1988, 81–108; here consequences for market cycle prognoses are drawn from observations of noncyclical movements. In all probability, the so-called GARCH (Generalized Autoregressive Conditional Heteroscedasticity) models for calculating volatility clusters and shareholder returns must be counted among such efforts to bring nondeterministic knowledge forms into line with determinism. In these models, variance is calculated not only according to the history of temporal sequences but also as a function of its own history and the history of random errors.

   13. See Chapter 1, n.11; Fox, *Myth of the Rational Market*, 233; Mandelbrot and Hudson, *(Mis)behavior of Markets*, 4. See also R. Lewinson and F. Pick, *La*

bourse. Les diverses formes de la speculation dans les grandes bourses mondiales, Paris 1938, 7.

14. Rifkin, *Access*, 44–45.

15. Friedman, *Capitalism and Freedom*, 14. John Stuart Mill has this to say about the merely veiling character of money:

It is not with money that things are really purchased. Nobody's income (except that of the gold or silver miner) is derived from the precious metals. The pounds or shillings which a person receives weekly or yearly, are not what constitutes his income; they are a sort of tickets or orders which he can present for payment at any shop he pleases, and which entitle him to receive a certain value of any commodity that he makes choice of. . . . There cannot, in short, be intrinsically a more insignificant thing, in the economy of society, than money. (John Stuart Mill, *Principles of Political Economy*, vol. 2, London 1848, 9)

16. Hyman P. Minsky, *Stabilizing an Unstable Economy*, New Haven 1986, 119.

17. Hyman P. Minsky, *Can "It" Happen Again? Essays on Instability and Finance*, Armonk 1982, 91; *The Financial Instability Hypothesis. A Restatement*, London 1978, 1–3; see John Maynard Keynes, *The General Theory of Employment, Interest and Money*, New York 1936.

18. De la Vega, *Die Verwirrungen der Verwirrungen*, 65. On the self-reflexiveness of financial markets, see Soros, *Crisis of Global Capitalism*, 8, 70ff; George Soros, *Open Society. Reforming Global Capitalism*, New York 2000, 58ff.

19. Immanuel Kant, *Critique of the Power of Judgment*, trans. Paul Guyer and Eric Matthews, Cambridge 2000, 124.

20. Keynes, *General Theory*, 156; Robert Skidelsky, *Keynes. The Return of the Master*, New York 2009, 83, 93. See André Orlean, *Le pouvoir de la finance*, Paris 1999, 32–62; on the thoroughgoing replacement of "rational explications equilibria" by "rational belief equilibria," see Mordecai Kurz, *Endogenous Uncertainty and Rational Belief Equilibrium: A Unified Theory of Market Volatility*, Stanford University, July 14, 1999 (http://www.stanford.edu/mordecai/OnLinePdf/13.UnifiedView_1999.pdf).

21. Gabriel Tarde, *Psychologie économique*, vol. 1, Paris 1902, 65; see Bruno Latour and Vincent Lépinay, *The Science of Passionate Interests*, Chicago 2009. This immanent pressure to conform may perhaps explain the neoliberal identification of money markets with an "economics of free speech": in both cases, rules are adopted which have "favorable effects on people's attitudes and beliefs and expectations," causing occasional idiosyncrasies in the movement of normative reinforcements and the mainstream to disappear. See Friedman, "Should There Be an Independent Monetary Authority?" in *Essence of Friedman*, 443; "Economics of Free Speech," ibid., 9–17.

22. Hyun Song Shin, *Risk and Liquidity*, Oxford 2010, 1–6; see Cassidy, *How Markets Fail*, 299–301.

23. Minsky, *Stabilizing and Unstable Economy*, 171–220; "The Financial Insta-bility Hypothesis: Capitalist Process and the Behavior of the Economy," in *Financial Crises: Theory, History and Policy*, ed. Charles P. Kindleberger and Jean-Pierre Lafargue, Cambridge MA 1982, 13–39; *The Financial Instability Hypoth-esis: A Restatement*, London 1978; *Financial Instability Revisited: The Economics of Disaster. Prepared for the Steering Committee for the Fundamental Reappraisal of the Discount Mechanism Appointed by the Board of Governors of the Federal Reserve System*, Washington 1970. See on this and on what follows: Riccardo Bellofiore and Piero Ferri (eds.), *Financial Keynesianism and Market Instability. The Eco-nomic Legacy of Hyman Minsky*, vol. 1, Cheltenham 2001, 1–30; Cassidy, *How Markets Fail*, 205–12; Thomas Strobl, *Minsky'sche Momente*, Jan. 2008 (http://www.weissgarnix.de/2008/01/01/minsky/).

24. Minsky, *Stabilizing an Unstable Economy*, 280, 6. It may briefly be noted here that an analogous movement, in which financing success proceeded by in-built recursions to a catastrophic fall, was extensively documented for the finan-cial world shaped by the Black-Scholes formula. After expanding at a terrific rate and posting impressive returns, the finance company Long Term Capital Man-agement was declared bankrupt not long after its cofounders, Merton and Scho-les, were awarded the Nobel Prize for Economics. The affair prompted one of the first big federal rescue packages in the US financial system; see Dunbar, *Inventing Money*; MacKenzie, *Engine, Not a Camera*.

25. On the paradox of liquidity, see Orlean, *Le pouvoir de la finance*, 33 and passim; Christian Marazzi, *Capital and Language: From the New Economy to the War Economy*, Cambridge/MA 2008, 24ff., 126.

26. Cited in André Orlean, *De l'euphorie à la panique: Penser la crise financère*, Paris 2009, 46. See also, in particular, Cassidy, *How Markets Fail. The Econom-ics of Rational Irrationality*, New York 2009, 251–316; Michel Aglietta and Sandra Rigot, *Crise et rénovation de la finance*, Paris 2009, 17–47.

27. Ralf Heidenreich and Stefan Heidenreich, *Mehr Geld*, Berlin 2008, 133.

28. According to the economist Gary Gorton, cited in Cassidy, *How Markets Fail*, 308.

29. See Shin, *Risk and Liquidity*, 4–13; Esposito, *Die Zukunft der Futures*, 225–39; Cassidy, *How Markets Fail*, 307–9; Michel Aglietta, *La crise. Pourquoi est-on arrivé là? Comment en sortir?*, Paris 2008, 17–31.

30. See Dirk Baecker, *Womit handeln Banken? Eine Untersuchung zur Risik-overarbeitung in der Wirtschaft*, Frankfurt/M. 1991, 11, 184.

31. John Maynard Keynes, *A Treatise on Probability*, London 1921, 20–40; see Skidelsky, *Keynes*, 84–86; Paul Davidson, "Risk and Uncertainty," in *The Eco-nomic Crisis and the State of Economics*, ed. Robert Skidelsky and Christian West-erlind Wigstrom, New York 2010, 13–29.

32. Luhmann, *Wirtschaft der Gesellschaft*, 171.

33. Esposito, *Die Zukunft der Futures*, 256.

34. Ibid., 256–57.

35. Ibid., 241, 252–55.

36. Orlean, *De l'euphorie à la panique*, 80.

37. Luhmann, *Wirtschaft der Gesellschaft*, 269.

38. Nicholas Taleb, *Fooled by Randomness*, New York: 2004, 249; see George L.S. Shackle, "The Science of Imprecision," in *Epistemics and Economics: A Critique of Economic Doctrines*, Cambridge, MA: 1972, 359–63.

39. Hans Blumenberg, *Lebenszeit und Weltzeit*, Frankfurt/M. 1986, 27.

40. Léon Walras, *Élements d'économie politique pure ou Théorie de la richesse sociale*, Paris 1900, 29.

41. Norbert Bolz, "Agenda Freiheit," *Merkur* 736/737, Sept./Oct. 2010, 892.

42. On this, see B. Latour and V. Lépinay, *The Science of Passionate Interests*, Chicago: 2009, 5; Jacques Sapir, *Quelle économie pour le XXIe siècle?* Paris: 2005, 407ff.

43. Luhmann, *Wirtschaft der Gesellschaft*, 270.

Cultural Memory | *in the Present*

François-David Sebbah, *Testing the Limit: Derrida, Henry, Levinas, and the Phenomenological Tradition*

Erik Peterson, *Theological Tractates*, edited by Michael J. Hollerich

Feisal G. Mohamed, *Milton and the Post-Secular Present: Ethics, Politics, Terrorism*

Pierre Hadot, *The Present Alone Is Our Happiness, Second Edition: Conversations with Jeannie Carlier and Arnold I. Davidson*

Yasco Horsman, *Theaters of Justice: Judging, Staging, and Working Through in Arendt, Brecht, and Delbo*

Jacques Derrida, *Parages*, edited by John P. Leavey

Henri Atlan, *The Sparks of Randomness, Volume 1: Spermatic Knowledge*

Rebecca Comay, *Mourning Sickness: Hegel and the French Revolution*

Djelal Kadir, *Memos from the Besieged City: Lifelines for Cultural Sustainability*

Stanley Cavell, *Little Did I Know: Excerpts from Memory*

Jeffrey Mehlman, *Adventures in the French Trade: Fragments Toward a Life*

Jacob Rogozinski, *The Ego and the Flesh: An Introduction to Egoanalysis*

Marcel Hénaff, *The Price of Truth: Gift, Money, and Philosophy*

Paul Patton, *Deleuzian Concepts: Philosophy, Colonialization, Politics*

Michael Fagenblat, *A Covenant of Creatures: Levinas's Philosophy of Judaism*

Stefanos Geroulanos, *An Atheism That Is Not Humanist Emerges in French Thought*

Andrew Herscher, *Violence Taking Place: The Architecture of the Kosovo Conflict*

Hans-Jörg Rheinberger, *On Historicizing Epistemology: An Essay*

Jacob Taubes, *From Cult to Culture*, edited by Charlotte Fonrobert and Amir Engel

Peter Hitchcock, *The Long Space: Transnationalism and Postcolonial Form*

Lambert Wiesing, *Artificial Presence: Philosophical Studies in Image Theory*

Jacob Taubes, *Occidental Eschatology*

Freddie Rokem, *Philosophers and Thespians: Thinking Performance*

Roberto Esposito, *Communitas: The Origin and Destiny of Community*

Vilashini Cooppan, *Worlds Within: National Narratives and Global Connections in Postcolonial Writing*

Josef Früchtl, *The Impertinent Self: A Heroic History of Modernity*

Frank Ankersmit, Ewa Domanska, and Hans Kellner, eds., *Re-Figuring Hayden White*

Michael Rothberg, *Multidirectional Memory: Remembering the Holocaust in the Age of Decolonization*

Jean-François Lyotard, *Enthusiasm: The Kantian Critique of History*

Ernst van Alphen, Mieke Bal, and Carel Smith, eds., *The Rhetoric of Sincerity*

Stéphane Mosès, *The Angel of History: Rosenzweig, Benjamin, Scholem*

Pierre Hadot, *The Present Alone Is Our Happiness: Conversations with Jeannie Carlier and Arnold I. Davidson*

Alexandre Lefebvre, *The Image of the Law: Deleuze, Bergson, Spinoza*

Jan Assmann, *Religion and Cultural Memory: Ten Studies*

David Scott and Charles Hirschkind, *Powers of the Secular Modern: Talal Asad and His Interlocutors*

Gyanendra Pandey, *Routine Violence: Nations, Fragments, Histories*

James Siegel, *Naming the Witch*

J. M. Bernstein, *Against Voluptuous Bodies: Late Modernism and the Meaning of Painting*

Theodore W. Jennings Jr., *Reading Derrida / Thinking Paul: On Justice*

Richard Rorty and Eduardo Mendieta, *Take Care of Freedom and Truth Will Take Care of Itself: Interviews with Richard Rorty*

Jacques Derrida, *Paper Machine*

Renaud Barbaras, *Desire and Distance: Introduction to a Phenomenology of Perception*

Jill Bennett, *Empathic Vision: Affect, Trauma, and Contemporary Art*

Ban Wang, *Illuminations from the Past: Trauma, Memory, and History in Modern China*

James Phillips, *Heidegger's* Volk: *Between National Socialism and Poetry*

Frank Ankersmit, *Sublime Historical Experience*

István Rév, *Retroactive Justice: Prehistory of Post-Communism*

Paola Marrati, *Genesis and Trace: Derrida Reading Husserl and Heidegger*

Krzysztof Ziarek, *The Force of Art*

Marie-José Mondzain, *Image, Icon, Economy: The Byzantine Origins of the Contemporary Imaginary*

Cecilia Sjöholm, *The Antigone Complex: Ethics and the Invention of Feminine Desire*

Jacques Derrida and Elisabeth Roudinesco, *For What Tomorrow . . . : A Dialogue*

Elisabeth Weber, *Questioning Judaism: Interviews by Elisabeth Weber*

Jacques Derrida and Catherine Malabou, *Counterpath: Traveling with Jacques Derrida*

Martin Seel, *Aesthetics of Appearing*

Nanette Salomon, *Shifting Priorities: Gender and Genre in Seventeenth-Century Dutch Painting*

Jacob Taubes, *The Political Theology of Paul*

Jean-Luc Marion, *The Crossing of the Visible*

Eric Michaud, *The Cult of Art in Nazi Germany*

Anne Freadman, *The Machinery of Talk: Charles Peirce and the Sign Hypothesis*

Stanley Cavell, *Emerson's Transcendental Etudes*

Stuart McLean, *The Event and Its Terrors: Ireland, Famine, Modernity*

Beate Rössler, ed., *Privacies: Philosophical Evaluations*

Bernard Faure, *Double Exposure: Cutting Across Buddhist and Western Discourses*

Alessia Ricciardi, *The Ends of Mourning: Psychoanalysis, Literature, Film*

Alain Badiou, *Saint Paul: The Foundation of Universalism*

Gil Anidjar, *The Jew, the Arab: A History of the Enemy*

Jonathan Culler and Kevin Lamb, eds., *Just Being Difficult? Academic Writing in the Public Arena*

Jean-Luc Nancy, *A Finite Thinking*, edited by Simon Sparks

Theodor W. Adorno, *Can One Live after Auschwitz? A Philosophical Reader*, edited by Rolf Tiedemann

Patricia Pisters, *The Matrix of Visual Culture: Working with Deleuze in Film Theory*

Andreas Huyssen, *Present Pasts: Urban Palimpsests and the Politics of Memory*

Talal Asad, *Formations of the Secular: Christianity, Islam, Modernity*

Dorothea von Mücke, *The Rise of the Fantastic Tale*

Marc Redfield, *The Politics of Aesthetics: Nationalism, Gender, Romanticism*

Emmanuel Levinas, *On Escape*

Dan Zahavi, *Husserl's Phenomenology*

Rodolphe Gasché, *The Idea of Form: Rethinking Kant's Aesthetics*

Michael Naas, *Taking on the Tradition: Jacques Derrida and the Legacies of Deconstruction*

Herlinde Pauer-Studer, ed., *Constructions of Practical Reason: Interviews on Moral and Political Philosophy*

Jean-Luc Marion, *Being Given That: Toward a Phenomenology of Givenness*

Theodor W. Adorno and Max Horkheimer, *Dialectic of Enlightenment*

Ian Balfour, *The Rhetoric of Romantic Prophecy*

Martin Stokhof, *World and Life as One: Ethics and Ontology in Wittgenstein's Early Thought*

Gianni Vattimo, *Nietzsche: An Introduction*

Jacques Derrida, *Negotiations: Interventions and Interviews, 1971–1998*, edited by Elizabeth Rottenberg

Brett Levinson, *The Ends of Literature: The Latin American "Boom" in the Neoliberal Marketplace*

Timothy J. Reiss, *Against Autonomy: Cultural Instruments, Mutualities, and the Fictive Imagination*

Hent de Vries and Samuel Weber, eds., *Religion and Media*

Niklas Luhmann, *Theories of Distinction: Re-Describing the Descriptions of Modernity*, edited and introduced by William Rasch

Johannes Fabian, *Anthropology with an Attitude: Critical Essays*

Michel Henry, *I Am the Truth: Toward a Philosophy of Christianity*

Gil Anidjar, *"Our Place in Al-Andalus": Kabbalah, Philosophy, Literature in Arab-Jewish Letters*

Hélène Cixous and Jacques Derrida, *Veils*

F. R. Ankersmit, *Historical Representation*

F. R. Ankersmit, *Political Representation*

Elissa Marder, *Dead Time: Temporal Disorders in the Wake of Modernity (Baudelaire and Flaubert)*

Reinhart Koselleck, *The Practice of Conceptual History: Timing History, Spacing Concepts*

Niklas Luhmann, *The Reality of the Mass Media*

Hubert Damisch, *A Theory of /Cloud/: Toward a History of Painting*

Jean-Luc Nancy, *The Speculative Remark: (One of Hegel's bon mots)*

Jean-François Lyotard, *Soundproof Room: Malraux's Anti-Aesthetics*

Jan Patočka, *Plato and Europe*

Hubert Damisch, *Skyline: The Narcissistic City*

Isabel Hoving, *In Praise of New Travelers: Reading Caribbean Migrant Women Writers*

Richard Rand, ed., *Futures: Of Jacques Derrida*

William Rasch, *Niklas Luhmann's Modernity: The Paradoxes of Differentiation*

Jacques Derrida and Anne Dufourmantelle, *Of Hospitality*

Jean-François Lyotard, *The Confession of Augustine*

Kaja Silverman, *World Spectators*

Samuel Weber, *Institution and Interpretation: Expanded Edition*

Jeffrey S. Librett, *The Rhetoric of Cultural Dialogue: Jews and Germans in the Epoch of Emancipation*

Ulrich Baer, *Remnants of Song: Trauma and the Experience of Modernity in Charles Baudelaire and Paul Celan*

Samuel C. Wheeler III, *Deconstruction as Analytic Philosophy*

David S. Ferris, *Silent Urns: Romanticism, Hellenism, Modernity*

Rodolphe Gasché, *Of Minimal Things: Studies on the Notion of Relation*

Sarah Winter, *Freud and the Institution of Psychoanalytic Knowledge*

Samuel Weber, *The Legend of Freud: Expanded Edition*

Aris Fioretos, ed., *The Solid Letter: Readings of Friedrich Hölderlin*

J. Hillis Miller / Manuel Asensi, *Black Holes / J. Hillis Miller; or, Boustrophedonic Reading*

Miryam Sas, *Fault Lines: Cultural Memory and Japanese Surrealism*

Peter Schwenger, *Fantasm and Fiction: On Textual Envisioning*

Didier Maleuvre, *Museum Memories: History, Technology, Art*

Jacques Derrida, *Monolingualism of the Other; or, The Prosthesis of Origin*

Andrew Baruch Wachtel, *Making a Nation, Breaking a Nation: Literature and Cultural Politics in Yugoslavia*

Niklas Luhmann, *Love as Passion: The Codification of Intimacy*

Mieke Bal, ed., *The Practice of Cultural Analysis: Exposing Interdisciplinary Interpretation*

Jacques Derrida and Gianni Vattimo, eds., *Religion*